Advance Praise for *Global Fishers: The Politics of Transnational Movements*

"*Global Fishers: The Politics of Transnational Movements* by Elyse Mills is a pathbreaking book about a very important but largely overlooked transnational social movement. It is a modern classic in the making. All academic researchers and activists interested in social justice and a positive future of humanity must read this book."

— Saturnino M. Borras Jr., co-author of *Political Dynamics of Transnational Agrarian Movements*

"*Global Fishers* offers an unparalleled historical account of one of the world's lesser known, but vitally important social movements. But Elyse Mills' book is more than a history of the transnational fishers' movements, it is also an insider account of political strategies, splits and struggles as they unfold to resist the ever-shifting forces of industrialization, privatization and extractivism. Essential reading for students of anthropology, development studies and politics who know that history is made as much from the bottom-up as it is from the top-down."

— Liam Campling, author of *Capitalism and the Sea* and professor of international business and development, Queen Mary University of London

"A powerful message about the past, present and future of global fishers' movements. This book advances our understandings of the politics of fishers' movements and, in so doing, offers important insights into the politics of fisheries and food systems more broadly. A must read for anyone working at the intersection of movements and food governance."

— Jessica Duncan, associate professor in the politics of food systems transformations, Wageningen University

"This is a very well researched and written book that will make an important contribution to the scholarship and practice of transnational fishers' movements and social movements more broadly. The text provides a valuable overview of two key network organizations at the centre of fishers' movements and traces their origins, development, and engagement in contemporary transnational political spaces."

— Charles Levkoe, Canada Research Chair in Equitable and Sustainable Food Systems and associate professor, Lakehead University

"Can we conceive food sovereignty and climate justice without the peoples from the lakes, rivers and oceans? Clearly not and yet we know little about them. This book is a groundbreaking contribution to fill this gap. It tells the story of the fisher peoples, their struggles and aspirations, and how they have organized to defend not just themselves, but our blue planet."

— Sofia Monsalve, secretary general, FIAN International

"This book fills an important gap in the literature on global politics and transnational social movements through its focus on small-scale fishers' movements."

— Kristen Lowitt, assistant professor, School of Environmental Studies, Queen's University

"Elyse Noble Mills has written the definitive account of transnational fishers' movements, such as the World Forum of Fisher Peoples (WFFP) and the World Forum of Fish Harvesters and Fish Workers (WFF). But this magnificent book is more than that, analyzing not just justice movements of small-scale fishers but also the varied global governance arenas that deal with ocean and inland aquatic resources, climate change, plummeting seafood stocks, and thorny issues of geopolitics, biodiversity, and intellectual property of genetic material. A remarkable tour-de-force!"

— Marc Edelman, Hunter College and the Graduate Center, City University of New York

"*Global Fishers: The Politics of Transnational Movements* is a fascinating book that should be essential reading for anyone interested in the world's small-scale fisheries, in social justice movements, and in big global issues of climate change and food security. Mills explores how these all interrelate, in an intriguing book that looks back in time, and forward, through the lens of the two major international fishers' movements."

— Anthony Charles, director, School of the Environment, Saint Mary's University

"Mills has crafted a clear, well organized and highly informative book describing the struggles, politics, aspirations and possibilities of the global "fisheries justice" movements. It is a 'must read' for students of history, food justice activists, and indeed for anyone who seeks to understand the critical link between small-scale fishers, food security, ecological health and climate change."

— Nettie Wiebe, farmer, founding leader of La Vía Campesina and professor emerita at St. Andrew's College, University of Saskatchewan

"In this empirically rich and carefully argued book, Elyse Mills analyses the structural conditions which shaped the transnational fishers' struggles for justice and recognition. She shows how activists were able to build and maintain through painstaking organizational work an effective movement, which not only defended fishers' interests but also contributed to food sovereignty and agrarian justice movements. This is essential reading for scholars and activists interested in social movements and environmental justice."

— Murat Arsel, professor of political economy, International Institute of Social Studies

"Millions of fishermen and women in developing countries undergo great hardship because of the waves of industrialization, privatization and conservation that have whipped their industries. In response, however, they have organized themselves and fought battles to defend their ways of life. This book provides a thoughtful analysis of the backgrounds and the political strategies of the most important international fishers' movements of this moment. The author must be congratulated for contributing a timely account of this overlooked corner of global food politics."

— Maarten Bavinck, professor of coastal resource governance, University of Amsterdam

Global Fishers

ALSO IN THE CRITICAL DEVELOPMENT STUDIES SERIES

Tiny Engines of Abundance: A History of Peasant Productivity and Repression (2022)
By Jim Handy

COVID-19 and the Future of Capitalism: Postcapitalist Horizons Beyond Neo-Liberalism (2021)
By Efe Can Gürcan, Ömer Ersin Kahraman & Selen Yanmaz

Extractivism: Politics, Economy and Ecology (2021)
By Eduardo Gudynas

The Political Economy of Agrarian Extractivism: Lessons from Bolivia (2020)
by Ben M. McKay

Development in Latin America: Toward a New Future (2019)
by Maristella Svampa, translation by Mark Rushton

Politics Rules: Power, Globalization and Development (2019)
by Adam Sneyd

Critical Development Studies: An Introduction (2018)
by Henry Veltmeyer & Raúl Delgado Wise

Global Fishers

The Politics of Transnational Movements

ELYSE NOBLE MILLS

CRITICAL DEVELOPMENT STUDIES

Copyright © 2022 Elyse Noble Mills

All rights reserved. No part of this book may be reproduced or transmitted in any form by any means without permission in writing from the publisher, except by a reviewer, who may quote brief passages in a review.

Editing: Brenda Conroy
Cover photo: Elyse Mills, WFFP 7th General Assembly
Design: John van der Woude, JVDW Designs
Printed and bound in Canada

Published in North America by Fernwood Publishing
2970 Oxford Street, Halifax, Nova Scotia, B3L 2W4
and 748 Broadway Avenue, Winnipeg, Manitoba, R3G 0X3
www.fernwoodpublishing.ca

Published in the rest of the world by Practical Action Publishing
27a Albert Street, Rugby, Warwickshire CV21 2SG, UK

Fernwood Publishing Company Limited gratefully acknowledges the financial support of the Government of Canada through the Canada Book Fund and the Canada Council for the Arts, the Nova Scotia Department of Communities, Culture and Heritage, the Manitoba Department of Culture, Heritage and Tourism under the Manitoba Publishers Marketing Assistance Program and the Province of Manitoba, through the Book Publishing Tax Credit, for our publishing program.

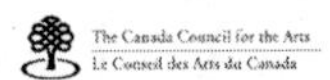

Library and Archives Canada Cataloguing in Publication

Title: Global fishers : the politics of transnational movements / Elyse Noble Mills.
Names: Mills, Elyse Noble, author.
Series: Critical development studies ; 8.
Description: Series statement: Critical development studies ; 8 | Includes bibliographical references and index.
Identifiers: Canadiana (print) 20220498008 | Canadiana (ebook) 20220498067 | ISBN 9781773635941
(softcover) | ISBN 9781773636160 (EPUB) | ISBN 9781773636177 (PDF)
Subjects: LCSH: Fisheries—Political activity. | LCSH: Fisheries—Social aspects. | LCSH: Social
movements. | LCSH: World politics.
Classification: LCC SH331 .M55 2023 | DDC 338.3/727—dc23

Contents

Critical Development Studies Series

Three decades of uneven capitalist development and neoliberal globalization have devastated the economies, societies, livelihoods and lives of people around the world, especially those in societies of the Global South. Now more than ever, there is a need for a more critical, proactive approach to the study of global and development studies. The challenge of advancing and disseminating such an approach — to provide global and development studies with a critical edge — is on the agenda of scholars and activists from across Canada and the world and those who share the concern and interest in effecting progressive change for a better world.

This series provides a forum for the publication of small books in the interdisciplinary field of critical development studies — to generate knowledge and ideas about transformative change and alternative development. The editors of the series welcome the submission of original manuscripts that focus on issues of concern to the growing worldwide community of activist scholars in this field. Critical development studies (CDS) encompasses a broad array of issues ranging from the sustainability of the environment and livelihoods, the political economy and sociology of social inequality, alternative models of local and community-based development, the land and resource-grabbing dynamics of extractive capital, the subnational and global dynamics of political and economic power, and the forces of social change and resistance, as well as the contours of contemporary struggles against the destructive operations and ravages of capitalism and imperialism in the twenty-first century.

The books in the series are designed to be accessible to an activist readership as well as the academic community. The intent is to publish a series of small books (54,000 words, including bibliography, endnotes, index and front matter) on some of the biggest issues in the interdisciplinary field of critical development studies. To this end, activist scholars from across the world in the field of development studies and related academic disciplines are invited to submit a proposal or the draft of a book that conforms to the stated aim of the series. The editors will consider the submission of complete manuscripts within the 54,000-word limit. Potential authors are encouraged to submit a proposal that includes a rationale and short synopsis of the book, an outline of proposed chapters, one or two sample chapters, and a brief biography of the author(s).

Series Editors

HENRY VELTMEYER is a research professor at Universidad Autónoma de Zacatecas (Mexico) and professor emeritus of International Development Studies at Saint Mary's University (Canada), with a specialized interest in Latin American development. He is also co-chair of the Critical Development Studies Network and a co-editor of Fernwood's Agrarian Change and Peasant Studies series. The CDS *Handbook: Tools for Change* (Fernwood, 2011) was published in French by University of Ottawa Press as *Des outils pour le changement : Une approche critique en études du développement* and in Spanish as *Herramientas para el Cambio*, with funding from Oxfam UK by CIDES, Universidad Mayor de San Andrés, La Paz, Bolivia.

ANNETTE AURÉLIE DESMARAIS is the Canada Research Chair in Human Rights, Social Justice and Food Sovereignty at the University of Manitoba (Canada). She is the author of *La Vía Campesina: Globalization and the Power of Peasants* (Fernwood, 2007), which has been republished in French, Spanish, Korean, Italian and Portuguese, and *Frontline Farmers: How the National Farmers Union Resists Agribusiness and Creates our New Food Future* (Fernwood, 2019). She is co-editor of *Food Sovereignty: Reconnecting Food, Nature and Community* (Fernwood, 2010); *Food Sovereignty in Canada: Creating Just and Sustainable Food Systems* (Fernwood, 2011); and *Public Policies for Food Sovereignty: Social Movements and the State* (Routledge, 2017).

RAÚL DELGADO WISE is a research professor and director of the PhD program in Development Studies at the Universidad Autónoma de Zacatecas (Mexico). He holds the prestigious UNESCO Chair on Migration and Development and is executive director of the International Migration and Development Network, as well as author and editor of some twenty books and more than a hundred essays. He is a member of the Mexican Academy of Sciences and editor of the book series, Latin America and the New World Order, for Miguel Angel Porrúa publishers and chief editor of the journal *Migración y Desarrollo*. He is also a member of the international working group, People's Global Action on Migration Development and Human Rights.

*Dedicated to the members of the World Forum of Fisher Peoples
and the World Forum of Fish Harvesters and Fish Workers,
for their continuous commitment to a more just and equitable world.*

Acronyms

CBD	Convention on Biological Diversity
CC	Coordination Committee
CFI	Coastal Fisheries Initiative
CFP	Common Fisheries Policy
CFS	Committee on World Food Security
COFI	Committee on Fisheries
COP	Conference of the Parties
CSA	Climate-Smart Agriculture, Forestry and Fisheries
CSM	Civil Society and Indigenous Peoples Mechanism
CSO	Civil Society Organization
EEZ	Exclusive Economic Zone
EU	European Union
FAO	Food and Agriculture Organization of the United Nations
FIAN	Food First Information and Action Network
HLPE	High Level Panel of Experts
ICSF	International Collective in Support of Fishworkers
IFAD	International Fund for Agricultural Development
IFQ	Individual Fishing Quota
IIPFCC	International Indigenous Peoples Forum on Climate Change
IITC	International Indian Treaty Council
ILO	International Labour Organization
IPC	International Planning Committee for Food Sovereignty
IPCC	Intergovernmental Panel on Climate Change
ITQ	Individual Transferable Quota
LMPA	Large Marine Protected Area

LVC	La Vía Campesina
MDGS	Millennium Development Goals
MFU	Maritime Fishermen's Union
MPA	Marine Protected Area
NFF	National Fishworkers Forum
NFI	Fisheries and Aquaculture Division (FAO)
NGO	Non-Governmental Organization
OECD	Organisation for Economic Co-operation and Development
REDD+	reducing emissions from deforestation and forest degradation
SDGS	Sustainable Development Goals
SFPA	Sustainable Fisheries Partnership Agreement
SIDS	Small Island Developing States
SSF-GSF	Global Strategic Framework on the Small-Scale Fisheries Guidelines
SSF GUIDELINES	Voluntary Guidelines for Securing Sustainable Small-Scale Fisheries
TBTI	Too Big to Ignore
TNI	Transnational Institute
UN	United Nations
UNCLOS	United Nations Convention on the Law of the Sea
UNDRIP	United Nations Declaration on the Rights of Indigenous Peoples
UNDROP	United Nations Declaration on the Rights of Peasants and Other People Working in Rural Areas
UNFCCC	United Nations Framework Convention on Climate Change
VGFSYN	Voluntary Guidelines on Food Systems and Nutrition
WFF	World Forum of Fish Harvesters and Fish Workers
WFFP	World Forum of Fisher Peoples
WFP	World Food Programme
WG	Working Group
WTO	World Trade Organization
ZAC	Zone of Action for the Climate

1 Diving into the Politics of Transnational Fisheries Justice Movements

Transnational fishers' movements, like all social movements, have a history marked by both periods of politically charged, lively mobilization, and quieter moments, impacted by a lack of capacity, resources and organization. It is a history full of inspiring events, general assemblies, protests, alliance-building, convergences, internal and external tensions, conflicts and agreements, and social and political losses and gains. It is also a history that is difficult to piece together, due to the absence of complete or available archives. There are fragments of documentation here and there, mainly in the collections of individuals who have been part of the movements or of organizations that have worked closely with the movements. There are also vivid stories shared between long-term and newer members and allies and differing perspectives on how things played out in various meetings and processes. Much of the movements' historical fabric and organizational memory is preserved within the minds of the founding and early members and the members of allied organizations who have worked with the movements for many years. Some of this history has been lost along with members who have left the movements or passed away. However, ensuring that the history that remains is preserved, shared widely and learned from is crucial for the future viability of the movements.

Fishers' movements face the added complication of being embedded within the fisheries sector — a sector laden with complex and contentious politics, within which many conflicting interests are at play. New actors, issues and agendas are constantly emerging, making it difficult to have a clear picture of who is doing what and why. Particularly enigmatic is the role that social movements play in fisheries politics. This book bridges this gap by focusing on two transnational movements representing small-scale fishers — the World Forum of Fisher Peoples (WFFP) and the World Forum of Fish Harvesters and Fish Workers (WFF). It links the politics of these movements with academic and political debates by exploring three connected spheres: *transnational movements* contesting and seeking to influence the politics of global fisheries; *international political spaces* movements are prioritizing; and *contentious fisheries issues* movements are struggling over (Mills, 2021).

Despite being historically under-researched, fishers' movements and their political agendas have played a critical role in global fisheries, particularly in the context of rural and environmental transformations. These global transformations include rural spaces and food production expanding beyond farming and agriculture; climate politics moving to the forefront of global development processes; and international political arenas (such as the United Nations) increasingly illuminating the importance of transnational social movements (Borras et al., 2018). These transformations accentuate the critical need for fishers' organizations to mobilize beyond their national boundaries and expand their movements internationally. Exploring movements like WFFP and WFF gives us a more concrete picture and a better

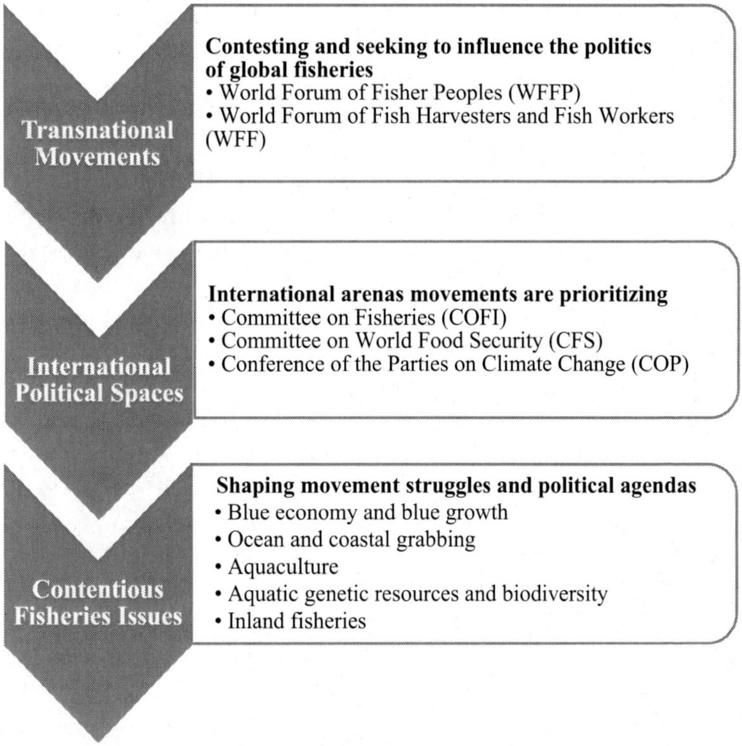

Transnational Movements

Contesting and seeking to influence the politics of global fisheries
- World Forum of Fisher Peoples (WFFP)
- World Forum of Fish Harvesters and Fish Workers (WFF)

International Political Spaces

International arenas movements are prioritizing
- Committee on Fisheries (COFI)
- Committee on World Food Security (CFS)
- Conference of the Parties on Climate Change (COP)

Contentious Fisheries Issues

Shaping movement struggles and political agendas
- Blue economy and blue growth
- Ocean and coastal grabbing
- Aquaculture
- Aquatic genetic resources and biodiversity
- Inland fisheries

understanding of the dynamics that are reshaping global political spaces and social movement politics (Mills, 2021).

Why Fishers' Movements Matter

In the last fifteen years, the politics around food systems — namely production, circulation and consumption — have gained widespread interest. Food systems became a particularly hot topic in the wake of the 2007–08 food price crisis, during which food prices around the world shot up rapidly, leading to increased hunger, poverty and social unrest. This crisis directed attention to the role of small-scale farmers and agrarian issues in the global food system, resulting in a remarkable expansion of research in this field (Clapp, 2014). In contrast, awareness of small-scale fishers' issues and perspectives has remained limited, in both research and political spheres. Small-scale farmers and transnational agrarian movements have been able to gain access to new avenues for engagement with policymakers, non-governmental organizations (NGOs) and researchers, which has contributed to broadening the visibility of prominent agrarian movements, such as La Vía Campesina (LVC)[1] (Edelman and Borras, 2016). Yet, their fisher counterparts, WFFP and WFF, remain less visible. Fishers are typically subsumed into "agrarian" or "peasant" categories, which is partly accurate in that, in some national contexts, fisheries is understood as a part of the agricultural sector. However, merging fisheries and agriculture limits our understanding of the unique and complex issues that fishers face. The comparative lack of public awareness of small-scale fisheries issues is also surprising considering the sector's crucial importance to global food security — contributing 66 percent of catches for human consumption and providing 90 percent of employment in fisheries (FAO, 2020c). This raises the question: why is so much less known about fishers' movements than their farming counterparts?

All three transnational movements (LVC, WFF and WFFP) were established in the 1990s, partially in response to the ramping up of international food trade and the 1995 establishment of the World Trade Organization (WTO) (WFF, 1997). Initially, most members of WFFP were part of WFF, as one consolidated international organization. However, internal political tensions caused a split in 2000 at the 2nd WFF General Assembly in Loctudy, France (discussed in Chapter 3). The Icelandic, French and North and South American members remained in WFF, while the members from Asia, Africa and Oceania, and a Canadian First Nations member formed the WFFP (Mills, 2022; Sinha, 2012). Public lists show that WFFP currently has 75 member organizations (WFFP, 2020a), while WFF has 44 (WFF, 2020a).

WFFP and WFF can be considered "fisheries justice" movements, meaning collective struggles of local, national and transnational alliances of small-scale fishers, fishing communities and their allies who are concerned with issues of inclusion, equity, human rights, democratizing access to and control of natural resources and the politics of climate change (Mills, 2018). WFFP considers itself

> a mass-based social movement of small-scale fisher people from across the world, founded by a number of mass-based organisations from the Global South. WFFP was established in response to the increasing pressure being placed on small-scale fisheries, including habitat destruction, anthropogenic pollution, encroachment on small-scale fishing territories by the large scale fishing fleets, illegal fishing and overfishing. (WFFP, 2020a)

WFF considers itself

> an international organization that brings together small scale fishers' organizations for the establishment and upholding of fundamental human rights, social justice and culture of artisanal/small scale fish harvesters and fish workers, affirming the sea as source of all life and committing themselves to sustain fisheries and aquatic resources for the present and future generations to protect their livelihoods. (WFF, 2020a)

Both movements have played an important role in political debates in global fisheries by advocating for the human rights and survival of small-scale fishers, raising critical issues and demanding space at decision-making tables. This book argues that it has become increasingly important to connect WFFP and WFF more directly to academic and political debates in order to expand and deepen our understanding of food systems and social movements, particularly in this era of climate change. The book explores how deeper analyses of the politics of transnational fishers' movements can 1) broaden the scope of food politics beyond land and agriculture by examining how small-scale fishers, fisheries resources and territories are entangled in food system transformations and how fishers' movements contribute to alternative approaches; 2) extend debates around climate politics through analyses of how environmental change and mitigation and adaptation initiatives are impacting small-scale fishers and fisheries and how fishers' movements respond to these impacts; and 3) strengthen existing bodies of fisheries research and analyses of fisheries politics by integrating knowledge, insights and alternatives from fishers and their movements (Mills, 2021).[2]

Considering the many forms small-scale fisheries take globally, including for example artisanal and subsistence, and the diversity within these categories, it is difficult to adequately address all of the specificities within a broad discussion on transnational movements and the politics of global fisheries. Yet, as Charles (2011) notes, small-scale fisheries do share a core set of characteristics, including the low-impact methods and the social and cultural role fisheries play in their communities — particularly in comparison to large-scale, industrial fisheries. These commonalities make it useful to explore small-scale fisheries collectively, with small-scale fishers making up one broad socio-economic group, especially in the context of international processes like fisheries governance, seafood production and trade.[3]

This book aims to contribute to understanding where and how organized fishers' movements are engaging in the politics of global fisheries and through what channels they are finding ways to participate in formal and informal governance spaces and processes. The approach used to carry out this study also contributes analytical tools and empirical information which help to expand our understanding of transnational fishers' movements as movements that both overlap with, but are also distinct from, transnational agrarian movements. Beyond academic debates, this book also offers analyses and insights for fishers' movements themselves into their own positions and contributions in political arenas and identifies ways forward for strengthening and expanding practical pursuits toward fisheries justice.

Framing and Doing Research on Movements

Situated within the field of international development, this book takes an interdisciplinary and crosscutting approach. It engages with insights from both social and political sciences, weaving together three core sets of literature: fisheries politics (e.g., fishing communities, fisheries governance, policy); food politics (e.g., small-scale producers, food systems, food sovereignty); and climate politics (e.g., climate governance, mitigation and adaptation, climate justice).[4] Concepts and debates emerging from these three sets of literature have been used as building blocks to develop a crosscutting analytical framework. In relation to transnational mobilization among fishers, understandings of social struggle, social movements and the strategies used to broaden social and political reach have been particularly crucial in this book (see Edelman and Borras, 2016; Tarrow, 2011; Tilly, 2004; Edelman, 2001). The emergence of social movements around the world signalled a change in the way ordinary people participated in politics. By the early

2000s, the term "social movement" was recognized globally as a call for popular action and a way to resist oppressive, unbalanced power structures. Movements came to be understood as inclusive organizations made up of members of different interest groups, such as food producers, workers, women, students and youth, who are all bound together by a common struggle, often stemming from the malfunctioning or lack of democracy in a specific political setting (Tilly, 2004).

Yet, as Diani (2015) argues, approaches to researching social movements have historically been opaque. He suggests three areas that need to be further developed: First, conceptions of movements need to move beyond being comprised only of people to include objects, moments, spaces, rallies, events and strategies. Second, more information needs to be collected on the evolution of movements over time and how changes affect engagement in collective action. This is a response to studies of movements often being done at a single point in time and extensive archives of their activities being hard to find. Third, more research needs to be done on the long-term impacts of virtual interactions in social movements. Part of the focus of this book — particularly in Chapters 3, 4 and 5 — has been to explore and develop these three areas in relation to fishers' movements. This includes looking into some of the main international political spaces the movements participate in and how these spaces have contributed to the movement-building process. Political spaces themselves are opportunities and channels through which civil society actors can attempt to influence the discourses, policies and decisions that affect them (Gaventa, 2006). For transnational movements, international spaces have become particularly important since the 1990s as the intensification of globalization has contributed to changing forms of power and opened up new governance arenas, which has consequently created new spaces for citizen action and engagement (Gaventa and Tandon, 2010; Scott, 2008; Edelman, 1999). As global governance arenas, particularly at the UN level, began shifting toward a more participatory approach, civil society actors seeking to influence policy and decision-making processes, increasingly recognized the strategic importance of engaging in international intergovernmental spaces (McKeon, 2017a).

Set within this framework of transnational movements and international political spaces, it was necessary to develop an approach that suited the global context of this research. Early in this research process, I discovered the lack of written historical information about transnational fishers' movements. There was no central movement archive, no published histories and little trackable online presence. However, I also quickly learned that everyone I talked to about the movements had stories to tell and perspectives to share about what had happened at different moments in the movements' history. I began to collect these stories and weave together a historical narrative.

The research process involved a combination of three complementary sets of methods — archival, virtual and in-person — which were used to collect both primary and secondary data. The archival methods involved reviewing and analyzing existing literature, policies, reports, meeting minutes, mailing lists, social media pages and other documents. The virtual methods involved tracking discussions, news and documentation about particular processes and events online, attending online meetings and webinars and conducting formal semi-structured interviews with key actors. Interviewees included members of fishers' and agrarian movements, researchers and representatives from NGOs and international organizations. The in-person methods involved engaging in participant observation at events, conducting both formal semi-structured and informal conversational interviews with key actors (same as above) and taking and collecting photos. All interview participants have been kept anonymous in order to respect the political sensitivity of the research. This combination of methods allowed more ground to be covered transnationally, facilitating the collection of a range of data at multiple places and times and addressing a necessity which has emerged out of the contemporary globalized context for researchers to expand their approaches and methodologies (Mendez, 2008). This approach also allowed me to gain important insights into the evolution and trajectory of the transnational fishers' movements that would have been difficult to uncover otherwise.

Positionality and Context

An important element of understanding how and why someone does a particular type of research is understanding the researcher's story. What sparked their interest? What steps led them to conceiving of the research, and later, conducting it? Before diving into the story of the fishers' movements that unfolds in the rest of this book, I first give a brief account of what sparked my interest, both politically and academically, in these movements and the politics surrounding fisheries. I grew up in the rural fishing community of Prospect Bay, just outside of Halifax in the eastern province of Nova Scotia, Canada. As a child, lakes and oceans were a regular part of my daily life. I spent my summers fishing and paddling around the lake behind my childhood home, catching "tickle fish" (small crayfish) and hermit crabs, and swimming in the cool waters of the Northumberland Strait at our family cottage. For dinner, we would often go to the local lobster pound or buy the freshest catch directly from the lobster fishers that docked a few minutes down the road. When I finished high school, some of my classmates became lobster fishers, usually because they inherited a licence from a relative. The local fishers were always a visible fixture in the community, either because you could see their colourful boats tethered to their buoys in one of the bays or because someone had been lost at sea during a storm. After the tragic Swissair 111 crash off the coast of Peggy's Cove in 1998, the fishers were the first to get in their boats and help comb the waters for possible survivors, with many of them suffering from lifelong trauma because of what they found.

A decade later, during my undergraduate program in international development studies at York University in Toronto, a course about civil society in Latin America led to an interest in social movements. In that course, I did research projects on mobilization among the *cocaleros* (coca producers) in Bolivia and on agency in small-scale fishing communities in Nicaragua. This fascination with social organization continued to grow during my undergraduate life, propelling me to apply for a master's program where I could explore this interest more deeply. The International Institute of Social Studies in the Netherlands offered just that, and I joined the Agrarian and Environmental Studies major in order to delve deeper into critical agrarian studies and debates around rural social movements — particularly agrarian movements. I soon noticed that fishers were rarely visible in debates about rural social movements. Even when mentioned in passing, as for example, allies of agrarian movements, fishers never seemed to be the key point of interest, nor was much understood about their politics or history.

In 2015, while working as a freelance researcher, I had the opportunity to join the Transnational Institute (TNI) team in Paris for the COP21 (UN Climate Change Conference), where the Paris Agreement was adopted. In another part of the city, there was a parallel people's assembly taking place (discussed in detail in Chapter 4), where TNI was part of a delegation of social movements and allied organizations that were conducting workshops and events. Together with WFFP and WFF, TNI co-organized events on blue carbon as a "false solution" for climate change and converging land and water struggles and filmed interviews with WFFP and WFF members for a documentary. This was my first opportunity to work with the fishers' movements, and this work continued through research on EU Fisheries Agreements (see Mills et al., 2017) and the beginning of my PhD project in 2016.

During my five-year PhD journey, I had many more exciting opportunities to collaborate with and learn more about the transnational fishers' movements. Some of the highlights were participating in the WFFP's 7th

General Assembly in New Delhi in 2017; conducting a project evaluation for WFFP in 2018; participating in a political training for the fishers' movements and the UN's Committee on Fisheries 33rd Session in Rome in 2018; and participating in the Civil Society Mechanism forum and the Committee on World Food Security 46th Session in Rome in 2019.[5] These experiences taught me a great deal about the politics of global fisheries and how fishers' movements navigate international forums, while also allowing me to develop invaluable relationships with many of the members and allies of transnational fishers' movements. This was crucial for carrying out this research, not only for being recognized as a researcher but also as an ally supporting the struggles of the movements.

My position as an "engaged researcher," who is both sympathetic to and critical of the movements being studied (Edelman, 2009), or a "scholar-activist," who conducts rigorous academic work that is explicitly connected to political projects or movements (Borras, 2016), was central in guiding my approach to this research. A scholar-activist approach is challenging and involves a constant balancing act in figuring out how emotionally or politically invested you can be in your research and the people you engage with, as well as when to establish boundaries. A wise person who has worked with social movements for decades once told me that there are typically four types of researchers who engage with movements:

1) those who work closely with the movement, often taking on a staff role within the movement to support it from the inside. They often only publish what they see as beneficial to the movement;
2) those who are considered an ally and are invited by the movement to work on a particular project for short periods of time or to contribute their expertise on a particular issue;
3) those who are sympathetic to the movement but are autonomous enough to offer constructive criticism on how things are functioning as a way to possibly strengthen its agenda; and
4) those who are completely autonomous from the movement, conducting observational research from a distance, but are occasionally invited by the movement to participate in events or discussions.

As someone who moves between the second and third types, my role fluctuated at different moments during the research process. At times I felt conflicted about setting boundaries and about my alignment with the political struggles of the actors and movements I work with. Questions arose about how constructively critical I should or could be and what information could be revealed in order to avoid negatively impacting the actors and movements involved or their political relationships. There is no handbook for addressing such questions, so I dealt with these using social and political intuition, as well as advice from colleagues and mentors who had experience with similar situations. I also had many conversations with people engaging in or with fishers' movements to get a sense of what kind of critical analysis they found most useful to include in the research. These conversations served as important guideposts throughout the research process.

Organization of the Book

This book consists of six chapters, including this introductory chapter and a conclusion. Chapter 2 sets the context and explores the historical development of global fisheries, arguing that there have been three distinct yet overlapping waves: the industrialization wave (post-1900), the privatization wave (post-1970) and the conservation wave (post-2000). The chapter provides a global and historical framing for the book, reflecting on structural and institutional transformations in fisheries in the last century, and situates the research within development studies debates. It also reflects on how the consequences of these waves have facilitated overlapping processes of exclusion in global fisheries.

Chapter 3 tracks the transnational movements that are contesting and seeking to influence the politics of global fisheries. It weaves together the histories of WFF and WFFP, exploring the steps that were taken toward building an international fishers' network between 1984 and 2000 and the movements' evolution between 2000 to 2020. The chapter turns to three pivotal developments, which offer critical insights into the movements' political agendas and alliance-building strategies. These include fishers' movements' internalization of overlapping fisheries, food and climate crises; convergences between fishers' movements and agrarian movements and platforms; and intergovernmental bodies increasing their attention to fisheries issues in their analyses and activities.

Chapter 4 maps the international political spaces that fishers' movements are prioritizing. These include three intergovernmental United Nations spaces focusing on fisheries, food and climate governance: the Committee on Fisheries (COFI), the Committee on World Food Security (CFS) and the Conference of the Parties (COP) to the UN Framework Convention on Climate Change (UNFCCC). The chapter looks particularly at the movements' strategies for participation in these spaces, the role of alliances and the challenges they face in their engagement.

Chapter 5 identifies the contentious fisheries issues that movements are struggling over. It focuses on five main issues highlighted by the International Planning Committee for Food Sovereignty's (IPC) Fisheries Working Group and how the movements have grappled with and addressed these issues. These include blue economy and growth, ocean and coastal grabbing, aquaculture, aquatic genetic resources and biodiversity, and inland fisheries. The chapter also explores how these issues are embedded within the overlapping waves of development discussed in Chapter 2. These waves and associated processes of exclusion have profound impacts on small-scale fisheries, emerging through the expansion of privatization in the industrial seafood system; the extension of "sustainable development" into fishing areas; the spread of climate change mitigation and adaptation initiatives; and the impacts of the COVID-19 pandemic.

The concluding chapter synthesizes the book's main findings and implications. These include overlapping processes of exclusion triggering and propelling transnational mobilization; fishers' movements' engagement with fisheries, food and climate politics and their contributions to international political spaces; and the key role fishers' movements play in raising the profile of the issues and threats small-scale fishers are facing globally. The chapter also pinpoints critical issues for fisheries, food and climate governance, and challenges and ways forward for fisheries justice activism.

NOTES

1. La Vía Campesina is an international grassroots movement established in 1993 that defends small-scale sustainable agriculture as a way to promote social justice and dignity. It currently has 182 member organizations in 81 countries (LVC, 2017).
2. For the purposes of this book, food, climate and fisheries politics refer to the formal and informal structures, practices and processes constituting food, climate and fisheries governance and the actors involved. For a more indepth discussion on the importance of fishers' movements in food, climate and fisheries debates, see Mills, 2021.
3. For the purposes of this book, "small-scale fishers" refers to people who fish to meet food and basic livelihood needs and/or are directly involved in harvesting, processing or marketing fish. They typically work for themselves, without hiring outside labour; operate in near shore areas; employ traditional, low-technology or passive fishing gear; undertake single day fishing trips; and are engaged in the sale or trade of their catches.
4. For a more in-depth discussion on how fishers' movements can be linked to these three core sets of literature, see Mills, 2021. The reference list also provides resources for further reading on these core themes.
5. The COFI, CSM and CFS are all discussed in detail in Chapter 4 on international political spaces.

2 Three Waves of Development in Global Fisheries

Industrialization, Privatization, Conservation

Global fisheries have undergone a continuous process of development in the last several decades as diverse actors search for more effective ways of managing fisheries resources, accumulating profits, conserving aquatic ecosystems and ensuring that generations of fishers have access to secure livelihoods. This process has also, directly and indirectly, impacted small-scale fisheries and motivated fishers to mobilize and build global solidarity networks. Development in global fisheries has included three important decisive areas, or historical waves: 1) industrialization wave (post-1900); 2) privatization wave (post-1970); and 3) conservation wave (post-2000). While each wave has its own distinct characteristics, they overlap, meaning their undercurrents have been internalized into successive eras. Each wave has introduced both technical and policy solutions aimed at addressing the consequences that emerged from the previous era. In some ways, the development of fisheries has been inevitable, given it is a sector that depends entirely on extracting resources from fluid, aquatic spaces, forever shifting, moving and changing. This constantly evolving context also means the governance of fisheries should be adaptable and flexible enough to take on new challenges. This, however, has not always been the case; many national fisheries sectors have stagnated, or even collapsed, under the weight of rigid policies and management tools that focus narrowly on profit-making, efficiency and streamlining production (Campling and Colás, 2021; Longo et al., 2015; Sundar 2012).

A widely shared perspective about inadaptability in fisheries governance is that we are now amid a global fisheries crisis, in which continuous, uncontrolled extraction in the sector has depleted fish stocks and critically damaged aquatic ecosystems. Many argue that the fisheries crisis stems directly from a process of industrialization in fisheries, which became prominent in the early 1900s and expanded significantly in the 1950s in the aftermath of World War II. Industrialization allowed for an intensification of fishing, both through the modernization of gear and due to the resources invested in expanding the sector (Finley, 2016). Fish were treated as a continuously regenerative resource that would perpetually meet the growing demand of consumers and industries. However, as some regions began to face declining fish stocks in the 1970s, the need emerged for stricter control over who was fishing and how much was being caught. This sparked the development of numerous privatization strategies in the 1970s and 80s, which largely meant dividing fisheries into measured quotas and designated spaces in which different types of fishing activities were permitted (Allison, 2001; Chuenpagdee et al., 2005).

After a few decades, it became increasingly clear that this governance approach was not easing the depletion of fish stocks but was actually exacerbating it by making seafood an increasingly valuable commodity (Campling and Havice, 2014). By 2000, attention turned to a more environmentally concerned conservation approach, which focused on protecting aquatic spaces and resources in order to ensure they were used sustainably and would continue to provide for years to come. This approach, however, had a neoliberal twist that centred around making profit from environmental protection; thus, the private sector was motivated to remain centrally involved (Barbesgaard, 2018). This current conservation era continues to be characterized by attempts to balance the urgency of a rapidly degrading aquatic environment, the growing consumer demand for seafood and the global economy's insatiable thirst for profit.

First Wave: Industrialization (post-1900)

The industrialization wave arguably had the most significant, enduring impact of the sector's historical eras, forever changing the character and structure of fisheries on a global scale. While this process happened at different moments in different national contexts, on different levels and under different political circumstances, the processes through which it took place had similar outcomes. While industrialization was already well underway in Europe and North America by the early 1900s and had already significantly changed fisheries in these regions by the 1920s, the post–World War II period was crucial. Butcher (2004) calls this period, in which industrial processes were significantly ramped up to boost economic recovery, "The Great Fish Race." Fisheries were dramatically transformed by unprecedented expansion.

Post-1950s growth in the fishing and seafood processing sectors rapidly became a global trend. A big part of this growth stemmed from the European invention of large-scale fish factory ships as part of the development strategy for post–World War II recovery. Although the use of these ships was pioneered by the United Kingdom, by the 1960s they were adopted by many other prominent fishing countries — Norway, Japan, Russia and Spain — which began replacing their small-scale fishing fleets (Mansfield, 2011; Finley, 2016). By the 1970s, the United States had also introduced large-scale processing ships into its fishing fleet. Today, industrial vessels are found around the world, but are most commonly used by European, North and South American, and East Asian countries. Some of these ships — which can reach lengths of up to 130 metres — not only catch fish but also process them on board, meaning they can stay out at sea for more than a year (Mansfield, 2011). The effect the industrial wave had on all three spheres of the sector (marine capture, inland capture and aquaculture) was huge — with production more than doubling, from 41 to 83 million tonnes, between 1961 and 1984 (Kurien, 2006). Along with the increased demand for fish as food and animal feed, one of the main reasons behind such rapid growth was corresponding advances in technology used for harvesting, processing and transportation. Countries that were already heavily industrialized by the 1960s, such as the United Kingdom and Canada, were the dominant players in production, providing around 60 percent (24 million tonnes) of seafood globally (Kurien, 2006).

The industrialization wave allowed the rapid spread of new industrial methods between diverse fisheries sectors worldwide, allowing more links and trade connections between them. Seafood is a unique commodity due to its high perishability when fresh (meaning not dried or salted). Once a fisher has caught three or four fish, the resulting surplus usually requires them to trade what their family cannot eat in a day or two. This makes trade intrinsic in fisheries. Around a third of all seafood production is routinely traded in the international market, making it the most traded primary food commodity globally. This level of trade has remained remarkably stable since the mid-1970s (Kurien, 2006). Along with the growing demand for industrial boats, high-tech equipment and seafood itself, research and development in fisheries also expanded rapidly. This contributed to the advancement of several new types of intensive fishing methods — the most used being trawling, purse-seining and longlining.[1] Such methods have remained at the heart of the industrial seafood sector, dominated by a few global firms hailing mainly from Japan, Russia, Norway, Thailand and the United States. Many of these companies also produce fish meal and oil, made of ground-up fish parts, which are added to animal feed and fertilizer used in industrial farming (Mansfield, 2011).

Exporting the Industrial Agenda

Alongside trade and development, fisheries management policies and governance approaches directly and indirectly facilitated mainstreaming and exporting the industrial agenda from the Global North to the Global South. One example is the European Union's Common Fisheries Policy (CFP), which was developed in the 1970s and formally established in 1983. The CFP sets out the central legal framework for all fisheries management and regulation — both inside and outside EU waters. A central element of the CFP involves giving government subsidies to large-scale EU-flagged fishing fleets, which essentially fund their capacity to sail deeper into foreign waters (Mills et al., 2017). The CFP also includes several policies and regulations directed toward non-EU governments — such as sustainable fisheries partnership agreements (SFPAs) — that aim to promote the EU's agenda. The establishment of SFPAs was largely due to overfished stocks in European waters, which meant that EU fishing fleets were no longer able to meet domestic seafood demands. SFPAs allow EU-flagged fishing fleets access to foreign waters in exchange for financial investment and technical support in host countries' domestic fisheries sectors. The EU is typically supposed to pay a lump sum for access rights, while also funding the development of more sustainable fisheries in the host country, such as through conservation projects. As of 2022, the EU has active agreements with 13 countries (11 of which are in Africa), which collectively receive more than €152 million annually; in some cases this is the main source of revenue for the host countries' fisheries ministries (European Commission, 2022; Mills et al., 2017).

The industrialization of fisheries exhibits five prominent features, the first of which is the enormous scale of today's fishing industry, which includes massive seafood companies, ships, nets and lines, and high-tech technologies. Second, global commodity chains provide consumers, particularly in the Global North, with a wide variety of fresh fish. Third, government policies promote the industrialization of fisheries by prioritizing modernization and development, treating fish primarily as economic resources and offering incentives to fishers to catch and sell more. Fourth, industrial fisheries contribute to the widespread displacement of small-scale and artisanal fisheries, sectors that are generally organized in a more sustainable and equitable way. And fifth, the capital-intensive fishing industry faces an inherent contradiction: its dependence on natural resources and simultaneous avoidance of functioning sustainably or paying environmental protection costs (Mansfield, 2011). These five features result in industrial fisheries essentially destroying the natural environment they depend on — as well as small-scale fisheries — in order to continue to expand and increase profitability. This contributes to imbalances in fisheries development, in which wealth distribution and consumption of resources within the sector are largely concentrated in the hands of owners of large industrial fishing companies. As the wealth of such companies grows, so too does their power in the fisheries sector, shifting some authority away from the state as the traditional decision-maker in fisheries governance. This has allowed private interests to become firmly rooted in the fisheries agenda, resulting in less attention to the protection of lives and livelihoods and accountability to the people working in the sector.

Snapshots: Industrialization in South Africa and India

In South Africa, an influx of British colonial capital financed a major transformation in marine fisheries between 1900 and 1920, influenced by the industrialization process in Britain's own fisheries sector a few decades earlier. By the mid-1930s, as the commercial fishing sector expanded rapidly, the national government introduced several new governance mechanisms, such as the individual quota system, which effectively further concentrated valuable marine resources in the hands of a few large (predominantly white-owned) fishing companies. During the post-World War II economic expansion period (1945–73), the shift toward export production further facilitated the accumulation of capital, fueled by an increase in international interest in South African fisheries. More and more foreign vessels appeared in its coastal waters, which meant small-scale South African fishers had to contend with increased competition, particularly for hake (a marine whitefish), which was growing in popularity in Europe. South Africa was only able to restrict foreign access to its national waters after its exclusive economic zone was established in 1977 (for more on this example, see Menon et al., 2018).

In India, the post-1947 independence period was characterized by rapid growth in urban areas, facilitated by the development of trade, industry and business. In the 1950s, government policies focused on rapidly expanding the trawling industry by building boatyards and harbours, hiring architects and engineers and investing in new technologies. Roads and railways in and around cities were also upgraded in order to make them more accessible and simplify seafood trade. Demand for seafood increased, and so did the prices. State planners focused on keeping up with the demand by increasing productivity in fisheries, seeing this as a way to address poverty — particularly in the small-scale sector. They pushed fishers to upgrade from traditional boats to more modern, industrial boats, which at the time were already being widely used in Europe and North America. The use of these new boats led not only to a significant increase in production, but also in input costs for fuel and boat and gear repairs. Small-scale fishers were not prepared for these costs, and many did not have the financial means to absorb them. New fisheries research, development and training institutions were also established across India, aiming to lead large-scale development programs in the sector – similar to those underway in countries such as Great Britain and Canada, with well-established industrial infrastructure. By the early 1960s, Indian fisheries had grown into a substantial export sector and today continues to play a key role in global fish trade (for more on this example, see Menon et al., 2018; Kurien, 1978).

Second Wave: Privatization (post-1970)

Many fisheries ministries and officials around the world considered the main issue stemming from the industrial wave to be the widespread, unchecked use of fisheries resources. Their interest in gaining more control over the resources and who had access to them contributed to the emergence of the privatization wave, in which many governments introduced private property–focused strategies and policies. Such initiatives were presented both to fishers and the general public as solutions for some of the environmental and social issues that emerged from the industrialization of fisheries. The justification was that more control over fisheries resources and areas meant that people would be less likely to abuse and overconsume resources, protecting stocks and ensuring they would remain for future generations of fishers (Longo et al., 2015).

Mainstream explanations for the depletion of fisheries resources typically stem from what Hardin (1968), a staunch defender of private property, calls the "tragedy of the commons." From this perspective, the lack of some form of private property or regulation inevitably leads to overfishing because when left unchecked, fishers will operate selfishly to serve their own interests. In other words, "freedom in commons brings ruin to all" (Hardin, 1968, 1248). This argument implies that fishers will always put their individual well-being ahead of that of their community or protecting the environment and are more likely to regulate the size of their catch if they have some sort of ownership rights (or economic incentive) over fish and fishing areas. The "tragedy of the commons" perspective suggests that as long as natural resources are part of a common pool, they will inevitably be depleted by greed and uncontrolled fishing activities. This argument has several limitations as it ignores important differences between small-scale and industrial fishing methods, the existence of community conservation and commons management strategies and the numerous political factors that influence fishing decisions. Ostrom's well-known work, for example, criticizes Hardin's argument, providing substantial theoretical and empirical evidence of how common-pool resources can be successfully managed without falling prey to individual greed. This could be done by designing resilient cooperative institutions that involve groups of resource users (such as fishers) who organize and govern small-scale common-pool resources themselves without top-down government intervention (Ostrom, 1990; Dietz et al., 2003).

Explaining overfishing as a simple case of the "tragedy of the commons" largely depoliticizes fisheries by blaming individual fishers for declining fish stocks rather than looking critically at structural issues and imbalanced power dynamics in the sector (Mansfield, 2011). Applying this perspective to the governance and control of the commons also facilitates particular outcomes and empowers certain actors at the expense of others. The growing concentration of capital and power in the hands of a few large fishing companies is largely ignored, as is the fact that such companies engage in a capital-intensive, labour un-intensive approach to fishing — meaning fewer people are able to access stable employment opportunities in the sector (Campling and Havice, 2014). The International Labour Organization (ILO) reports that, of the 35 million people worldwide engaged in capture fisheries, 37 percent have full-time employment, 23 percent work part-time, and the remaining 40 percent have either occasional employment or unspecified status (2021).

Longo et al. argue that Hardin's theory "is an inadequate framework for developing a deep understanding of socio-ecological dynamics and the historical contexts that influence the overexploitation of natural resources" (2015, 28). They assert that in oceans, fisheries and aquaculture, the situation can be better understood as a "tragedy of the commodity." This perspective focuses on how political-economic factors shape social organization and public life, addressing the activities and processes driving the commodification of all material things. Rooted in materialist conceptions of history and nature, in which the world is viewed as a series of material conditions, natural laws and phenomena, this approach explores the relationship between processes of production and consumption (socially and historically) and broader ecological conditions. The "tragedy of the commodity" highlights capitalism's dependence on continuous growth and the role that commodification plays in shaping the institutional rules that govern ecological systems — often labelled as commons. Contrary to Hardin's argument, these systems never exist in a state of free-for-all open access, entirely devoid of social organization, but are instead shaped by social conditions such as community traditions and norms. The environmental damage caused by open access is a manifestation of the tragedy of the commodity in that it stems from the continuous drive for capital accumulation and the relentless commodification of natural resources (Longo et al., 2015).

Introduction of Quota Systems

One of the most prominent developments emerging from the privatization wave was the establishment of "catch shares," or fishing quota systems — e.g., individual transferable quotas (ITQs) and individual fishing quotas (IFQs). ITQs and IFQs are types of catch shares used by many governments to regulate the use of fisheries resources and comply with fish stock limits established through the total allowable catch[2] (Bromley, 2009). Many governments and their fisheries departments considered quotas to be effective not only for limiting the size of fishers' catches but also to control who was fishing in their coastal waters. Quota systems, which were first introduced in the 1970s but popularized in the 1980s, are the most common type of private property scheme in global fisheries. They allow fishers to own access rights over a specific share or percentage of national fish stocks — creating property rights to access the fish but not for the fish themselves — with governments deciding both the total national catch and who gets the quotas (Mansfield, 2011). ITQ systems have been implemented in more than 20 countries globally and, accounting for about 20 percent of the total marine fish catch, are currently the most popular fisheries management approach (Costello and Ovando, 2019). However, there has been no evidence that quota systems have a direct impact on how much fish is actually being caught (Mansfield, 2011). An ITQ system also allows fishers to transfer their quotas by selling or leasing them to other fishers or fishing companies. This creates a competitive quota market in which large-scale industrial fleets are more economically equipped to buy up multiple quotas — granting them access to a significant percentage of the resources. When these quotas become concentrated in the hands of a few large companies, there is less access and fewer resources left over for small-scale fishers with less economic power (Jones et al., 2017; Levkoe et al., 2017; Longo et al., 2015; Sundar, 2012; Biswas, 2011; Isaacs, 2011).

Establishment of Exclusive Economic Zones

Another prominent development stemming from the privatization wave was the establishment of exclusive economic zones (EEZs). A core element of the 1982 *United Nations Convention on the Law of the Sea* (UNCLOS), EEZs allow governments to assert "ownership," or sovereignty, over their coastal waters, reaching 200 nautical miles from national coastlines. As a result, EEZs have enclosed approximately 90 percent of fishing grounds globally, with only 10 percent of marine fish being caught in international waters farther offshore (Sundar, 2012; UNCLOS, 1982; Campling and Colás, 2021; OECD, 2010). This makes the establishment of EEZs the longest single enclosure of natural resources and territory in history (Campling and Havice, 2014). The intention of these zones is that they would be used by fishers nationally but that foreign fleets may be permitted access to catch the surplus if a nation does not have adequate fishing capacity. To avoid such a surplus, many countries quickly expanded their fleets, which in many places ended up creating the opposite problem — overcapacity. Interestingly, many countries with low capacities have also used ITQs to transfer access to their EEZs to foreign fleets. Only the quota owner in this case benefits economically from what was once broadly considered to be a public good (Pinkerton, 2017). Thus, EEZs are no longer considered commons, or open access fishing grounds, but are transformed into state property. The ratification of UNCLOS gave governments the right to charge ground-rent (via fishing fees) to fishers for access to and use of fishing areas, as well as the power to determine the conditions of production by organizing how resources are managed and which groups of fishers are included or excluded (Campling and Havice, 2014; Campling and Colás, 2021). The establishment of quota systems and EEZs have been key turning points in the privatization process in fisheries, a process which has had long-lasting impacts in global fisheries and continues to evolve and emerge in various forms.

Snapshots: Privatization in Iceland and Chile

Iceland was one of the pioneers in implementing ITQs in its fisheries sector in the 1970s. In the mid-1980s, the quota system was expanded to encompass more fish species, and by 1991, was applied across Icelandic fisheries via the Fisheries Management Act. Quotas were established as assets with indefinite validity, which could be easily divided or transferred with minimal restrictions. Within a few decades, quota-managed fish, of which 19 species inhabit Iceland's EEZ alone, were responsible for 97 percent of the country's seafood harvest income. The main impacts of this system have been significant drops in new investment in fishing businesses, the number of operating vessels (particularly small-scale boats) and fishing efforts. During the early 2000s, Icelandic banks also acquired a large number of ITQs as collateral for loans, which ended up being a crucial element in the bank speculation that caused the country's economy to crash in 2009. By 2007, ITQs had become such a freely traded hot commodity, with banks readily handing out loans for quota acquisitions, that their total value had risen to 50 times the annual profit of the entire national fisheries sector. Shortly before the 2009 crash, some economists behind the establishment of the ITQ system noted that the privatization of the fisheries commons would inevitably negatively impact small-fisheries-dependent communities, arguing that their exclusion from the quota system was rational since they were not part of the "formal fishing industry." Small-scale fishers in the country have shown strong resistance to privatization in the sector, arguing that it is unethical, immoral and evil because of how the process prioritizes capital accumulation, individualism and private ownership over fishers' labour, livelihoods and collective well-being (for more on this example, see Arnason, 2005; Pinkerton, 2017; Jentoft, 2019).

Chile, one of the largest seafood producers in the world, has diversified its fisheries to include a multi-species industrial sector, a small-scale artisanal sector and a large-scale aquaculture sector. The government began privatizing marine fisheries in the 1970s and 80s, which in combination with the demarcation of its national 200-mile EEZ, facilitated rapid property and wealth concentration in the fisheries sector. The main beneficiary of this concentration has been the Anacleto Angelini group, which is estimated to control around 70 percent of Chile's northern industry. At first, Chile permitted foreign ships to fish in its southern waters off the coast of Patagonia where no Chilean fishers were working. However, as the domestic fleet expanded, it gradually took over the southern grounds as well. The first ITQs were established in the 1990s, with several key species being placed under quota management by the mid-1990s. Quotas, which typically have a duration of ten years, are initially allocated via auctions, and ownership is restricted to Chilean citizens and companies registered in the country. With an annual catch of 2.3 million tonnes in 2019, the development of the Chilean system represents a major expansion in the scope of fisheries quota management globally. The rapid spread of privatization measures in the sector has put enormous pressure on fish stocks, leading to the collapse of the mackerel fishery in 1998 and widespread protests by artisanal fishers frustrated by the unbalanced distribution of ITQs (for more on this example, see Ibarra et al., 2000; Arnason, 2002).

Third Wave: Conservation (post-2000)

While fishing continued to intensify and resources steadily declined during the privatization wave, it became increasingly apparent that the strategies that had been introduced to conserve resources had been far from effective. Overfishing and environmental degradation were still rampant and were becoming an ever pressing issue for the future viability of fisheries. Framed by a discourse of environmental protection, sustainability and climate change mitigation, the conservation wave emerged with the new millennium and intergovernmental promises to tackle global issues head-on. The UN's eight Millennium Development Goals (MDGs) set an agenda for the 2000–15 period, focusing on eradicating extreme poverty and hunger (Goal 1), ensuring environmental sustainability (Goal 7) and developing a global partnership for development (Goal 8), among other issues (UN, 2000). These goals were criticized for being relatively narrow in scope, focusing mainly on poverty eradication and improving human development (Gasper et al., 2019). They were also largely an initiative propelled by wealthy countries in the Global North, which, via institutions like the UN, the World Bank and the Organisation for Economic Co-operation and Development (OECD), acted as donors providing development assistance to the Global South. In the early 2000s, this form of donor support was a core element of "development" and an important source of income for many countries. However, by 2012 this importance had dwindled (Gasper, 2019).

The pursuit of the MDGs became significantly complicated by the "Great Recession" of 2007–08 and the subsequent convergence of food, feed and fuel crises. In combination with rapid growth and development in China and India, global dynamics of capital accumulation and patterns of food production, consumption and trade were significantly altered. Rapid growth also facilitated changing dietary preferences, contributing to the steady rise in global demand for animal protein (Weis, 2007). Global consumption of seafood grew exponentially — almost doubling, from 11.5 kilograms per capita in 1980 to 20.5 in 2020 (FAO, 2020c; 2012) (see Figure 2.1). Demand in North America and Europe was particularly noteworthy, with the highest seafood consumption per capita in the world (Mansfield, 2011). Eating more fish and "pescatarianism" — eating fish as your only source of animal protein — has become particularly popular in the Global North, due to both health warnings and environmental concerns surrounding eating red meat and industrially farmed animals (Ronquest-Ross et al., 2015). As growing demand and consumption put an increasing strain on available fisheries resources in the last two decades, governments have been ramping up

Figure 2.1 Global Fish Consumption

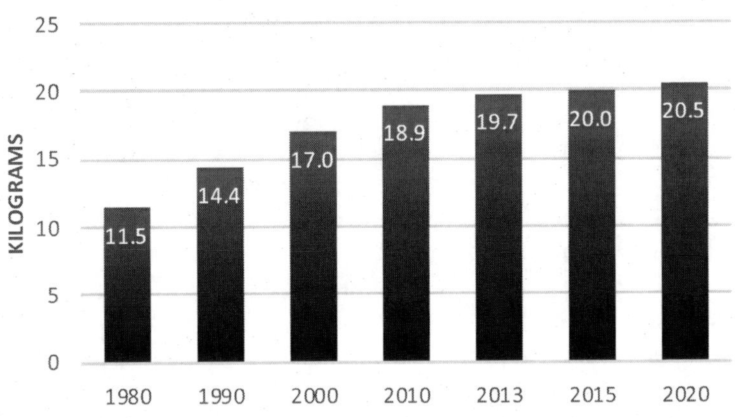

Source: author (using FAO 2012; 2020c data).

conservation strategies. The goal is not only environmental protection but also to protect the future viability of the fishing industry, which contributes to national economies, provides employment and supplies a crucial source of protein for local, national and international food systems. As part of this strategy, the 8 MDGs morphed into 17 Sustainable Development Goals (SDGs) in 2015, of which "Life Below Water" (Goal 14) became a key focal point for fisheries and marine conservation (UN, 2015a).

Enlargement of Marine Protected Areas

A key development of the conservation wave has been the enlargement of marine protected areas (MPAs). Fishing areas are increasingly being enclosed through the implementation of MPAs, in which governments enforce restrictions on fishing activities in places considered ecologically important or fragile — which often means coastal areas used by small-scale fishers (Campling et al., 2012). While various forms of protected areas have existed for hundreds of years, statutory MPAs are quite recent, with just 118 established by 1970, 430 by 1985, and 1306 by 1994. By the 1990s there were MPAs on virtually every coast; however, the majority only existed on paper due to a lack of financial and technical resources to ensure they were effectively managed. Most of these were implemented in coastal areas, where protecting fragile coral reefs and breeding grounds for many aquatic species was the priority (Kelleher et al., 1995).

The conservation wave fostered a new approach to establishing and managing MPAs, with a shift toward large marine protected areas (LMPAs), including those 30,000 km^2 and larger, and a push toward an international target of protecting 10 percent of the world's oceans by 2020 (Mallin et al., 2019). This goal was later increased to 30 percent by 2030 — also referred to as the 30x30 campaign (Marine Conservation Institute, 2022). The process of enlarging MPAs began in 2000 with the designation of the Northern Hawaiian Islands Coral Reef Ecosystem Reserve — initially a 360,000 km^2 area that was expanded to 1.5 million km^2 in 2006 and re-designated as the Papahānaumokuākea Marine National Monument. By 2013, the seven pioneer LMPAs alone accounted for more than 80 percent of the total area contained in protected areas (Wilhelm et al., 2014). Currently, around 7.4 percent (26.9 million km^2) of the world's oceans are protected within 16,928 MPAs — a tenfold increase since 2000 (Protected Planet, 2020).

Expansion and Intensification of Aquaculture

The aquaculture industry, or "culture fisheries," has also expanded drastically during the conservation wave, becoming one of the fastest growing food production sectors globally. While forms of small-scale traditional and Indigenous fish farming have existed for centuries, the expansion of large-scale intensive aquaculture, which depends on advanced technologies and enormous capital investment, has contributed to significant transformations in seafood production. This expansion has been propelled by economic interests and investment, which proponents claim are necessary to keep up with the increasing demand for seafood, which has not been matched by growth in capture fisheries. Between 1980 and 2018, while capture fisheries grew from 67 to 96 million tonnes per year, aquaculture production increased from 5 to 82 million tonnes — providing 52 percent of seafood for human consumption (FAO, 2020c) (see Figure 2.2).

Such rapid growth has allowed governments and the private sector to legitimize the industry as a more lucrative and predictable alternative to the capture fisheries sector. It has been heralded as a catch-all solution for numerous issues plaguing the fisheries sector, such as meeting global seafood demand, creating employment, addressing overfishing and supporting sustainability and the conservation of marine ecosystems by decreasing pressure on wild fish stocks (Ocean Foundation, 2020; World Bank, 2013). These claims have contributed to the rapid uptake of aquaculture around the world, from Norway to Myanmar, and Chile to Canada. This mainstreaming has even led to the development of the first genetically modified animal for human consumption — referred to as the AquAdvantage salmon by its

Figure 2.2 Global Aquaculture Production

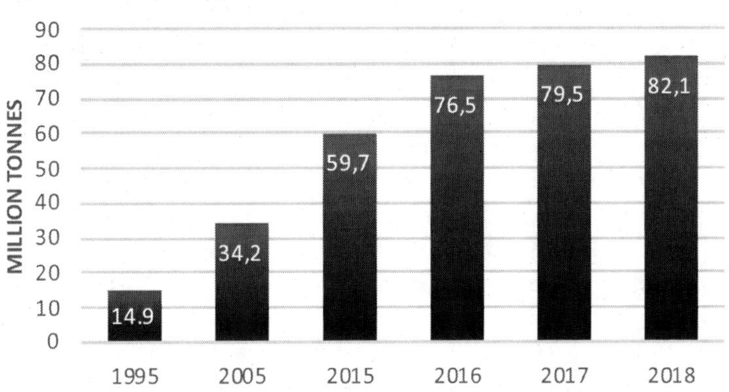

Source: author (using FAO 2020c data).

promoters, and "frankenfish" by its critics — which ironically won *Time* magazine's Best Inventions of 2010 award. The breeding of genetically modified salmon in aquaculture tanks has been promoted as a way to provide economic growth while ensuring ecological sustainability — representing the new holy grail of environmental solutions (Longo et al., 2015).

Snapshot: Aquaculture in Norway

Between 1995 and 2016, Norway's aquaculture production increased by 500 percent – making it the world's largest producer and exporter of farmed salmon. In 2016, its aquaculture sector made €7.4 billion in profit, accounting for around 8 percent of the country's total exports. As aquaculture companies outgrew the limits of the Norwegian coast, they began transporting their technologies and practices to other countries, such as Canada. By 2018, about 94 percent of the Norwegian aquaculture industry was producing farmed salmon, and the government still plans to increase production by a further 500 percent by 2050. This planned growth, however, requires public consultation, since coastal communities technically have a say in which potential production sites the industry has access to. There is a noticeable divide in public opinion among Norwegians. While some see it as a flourishing industry supporting the national economy, others are concerned that multinational companies are pushing small family companies out of the fisheries sector. Some conflicts have also emerged in communities where coastal space is being encroached upon. Another common fear is that such intensive industrial production will cause irreversible damage to marine ecosystems. One of the biggest environmental issues is the spread of sea lice, a parasite that kills an estimated 50,000 salmon in Norway per year. Sea lice breed rapidly in aquaculture tanks, spreading quickly between farmed fish and being transferred to wild salmon that swim near the tanks, or pick them up from the more than 200,000 salmon that escape from the tanks every year (for more on this example, see Krøvel et al., 2019; Castle, 2017; Longo et al., 2015).

Overlapping Waves and Processes of Exclusion

The combined consequences of the industrialization, privatization and conservation waves have led to overlapping processes of exclusion in the fisheries sector. The first process emerges from the technological advances of the late-19th century, which drastically transformed production and consumption patterns. By the 1950s, the amount of capital and resources being invested in fisheries had risen dramatically, facilitating the further advancement of fishing boats and gear capacities. This advancement led to the rapid expansion of large-scale industrial fishing operations engaging in highly mechanized fishing methods, which disrupted marine ecosystems and required less human labour. As demand for seafood accelerated between 1950 and 2000, the amount of fish caught globally quadrupled, from 20 to 90 billion kilograms (Longo et al., 2015).

The industrial wave has had numerous environmental, social and economic consequences, including a massive decline in fish stocks, biodiversity loss and livelihoods insecurities. A central feature of this period was the increasingly extractive nature in which fisheries resources were being harvested. Fishing was no longer only about supplying food to the global population but about extracting fisheries resources for profit. The contradictions inherent in industrial fisheries became increasingly apparent during this wave, as the sector became more and more dependent on a large supply of natural resources, while simultaneously exploiting these resources to critical levels (Campling et al., 2012). This illustrates the contradiction of the broader capitalist system, in which capital depends on its own continuous expansion into new domains in order to generate profit (O'Connor, 1998). The continuous expansion of the fisheries sector forced many fishers to adopt a "sink or swim" attitude — become profit-driven or risk being drowned by the competition. This mentality has allowed industrial fisheries to continue to thrive and grow, while overfishing and environmental decline run rampant. The result has been the near extinction of numerous species — such as large predatory fish (sharks, tuna, barracudas), of which 90 percent are estimated to have been lost globally (Clark and Clausen, 2008). Sea beds and corals have been dug up by trawlers; large marine animals have been snared by longlines and nets; and aquatic ecosystems have been polluted by oil and exhaust from boats. While large industrial fishing companies continue to fish as usual to expand their profits, fish stocks continue to plummet. The seas, lakes and rivers are increasingly underproducing, and as a result, new technological fishing gear is introduced to try to meet growing global demand (Campling et al., 2012).

Owners of industrial fishing companies employ several key strategies to increase their profits, including corporate concentration and centralization; using state subsidies to invest in large mechanized ships requiring relatively small crews; and precariously employing labourers, usually from lower-income countries (Campling and Colás, 2021). The ILO (2021) reports that more than 15 million people globally work full-time on board industrial fishing vessels, a large number of whom come from Southeast Asian countries like the Philippines, Thailand and Cambodia. At the same time, small-scale fishers are increasingly being pushed out of the sector, as governments prioritize the development of the economically lucrative industrial sector, while directing little investment or subsidies toward the small-scale sector. Many fishers who are no longer able to make a living fishing independently end up becoming hired labourers on industrial ships. Intensive industrial production has also oversaturated the market with cheap seafood, making it increasingly difficult for small-scale fishers to compete with prices and sell their catches. This has contributed to a significant rise in poverty among fishers globally and the deterioration of countless small-scale fishing communities, some of which have been completely deserted as people are forced to migrate in search of work (Mansfield, 2011; Béné, 2003).

These impacts continued into the subsequent privatization wave, in which small-scale fishers increasingly lost access to fishing areas and resources, and resources and power were further concentrated in the hands of large companies. Management strategies, such as quota systems, introduced during this wave failed to address industrialization-induced issues of overfishing and environmental destruction and exacerbated the intensity of fishing globally (Longo et al., 2015; Sundar, 2012). This wave also created significant controversy among fishers who were excluded from private property initiatives and faced even more obstacles to ensuring secure livelihoods and food security for their communities (Sundar, 2012; Isaacs and Witbooi, 2019). There was significant backlash from civil society groups who argued that fisheries resources and areas were being stripped from communities' hands and traditional users' access rights were being denied (Mills, 2018).

Tensions over how to address private property and fishing fees have been at the core of debates about the worsening fisheries crisis for decades, but these debates have more recently been reignited by growing attention to the essential role fisheries play in food security, the environment and development (Campling and Havice, 2014). A central reason why fishing communities and small-scale fishers have criticized and resisted privatization in fisheries is that initiatives such as quota systems are usually established by governments without providing space for communities to participate in their development or to propose their own approaches to sharing local resources. This also means that small-scale fishers are typically the first to lose out from such initiatives (Jentoft, 2019; Jones et al., 2017; Levkoe et al., 2017; Isaacs, 2011). Many small-scale fishers' organizations call for a human rights–based approach to resource access, which is centred around fishers' rights to secure livelihoods. A private property rights–based approach, on the other hand, only allows resources to be accessed by some individuals. Private property rights–based approaches to addressing overfishing focus on market efficiency, while causing social disruption in fishing communities by excluding many people who depend on fishing for their survival from accessing resources (Song and Soliman, 2019; WFFP et al., 2016; Ratner et al., 2014). Some fishers are forced to operate outside of the law, by fishing without a licence or quota, because they cannot afford the licensing fees, there are not enough quotas to go around or all the quotas have been snatched up by a few wealthy companies. This increases inequalities in fishing communities, with some fishers having to pay large fines or being unable to provide income and food for their families (Isaacs and Witbooi, 2019).

The second process of exclusion, stemming from the conservation wave, has exacerbated existing exclusion and tensions around accessing fisheries resources that emerged from industrialization and privatization. The predominant impacts of the conservation wave have been further exclusion of fishers from fishing areas, increasing division of fishing spaces for conservation purposes (such as via MPAs) and the intensification of capital accumulation through large-scale aquaculture production. These impacts have also been linked to broader processes of resource grabbing, in which fisheries resources and spaces are captured by powerful private and state actors. Such actors appropriate access to fisheries resources and spaces, while dispossessing previous users, rights holders and inhabitants with less economic and political power — such as small-scale fishers and coastal communities. Resource grabbing occurs via diverse mechanisms, including inadequate (inter)national governance and management approaches; trade and investment policies; coastal and marine conservation; and expansion of global food and fish industries, in which the rights and livelihoods of small-scale fishers are not sufficiently taken into account (TNI, 2014; Bennett et al., 2015; Bavinck et al., 2017). Despite justifications such as environmental protection, resource conservation, climate change mitigation and development, resource grabbing has largely been facilitated by mainstream approaches to fisheries governance that favour capital-intensive industrial capture and culture fisheries while subsequently marginalizing small-scale fisheries (TNI, 2014).

Overlapping processes of exclusion in global fisheries have facilitated significant transformations in the sector. These include rapid changes in the socio-economic relations of production that exist between fishers, markets and consumers, as large groups of fishers are excluded from markets and dispossessed of their means of production (fishing areas and resources) (Campling et al., 2012). Partly in response to these changes, fishers and coastal communities too are transforming as they find new ways to adapt to and survive within the sector. This has led to the emergence of different strategies of resistance and mobilization and the formation of transnational networks and movements. Such movements call dominant approaches to fisheries governance into question, arguing that they focus too narrowly on managing fisheries resources; gloss over the complex socio-political relations and dynamics that shape the fisheries system; and treat fishing communities as development subjects rather than powerful agents of change (Campling et al., 2012). Transnational fishers' movements have made important contributions to national and international fisheries governance by mobilizing and challenging the mainstream norms that neglect small-scale fishers' rights. In a global context in which the politics around the production, circulation and consumption of seafood are becoming increasingly complex and contentious, the role of fishers' movements in raising critical voices and challenging the status quo becomes all the more crucial.

NOTES

1. Trawling involves pulling a net behind a fishing boat, either through the water or along the seafloor. Purse-seining involves a round seine net that hangs vertically in the water from buoys on its top edge, while its bottom edge is held down by weights. The top edge is pulled closed to trap the fish. Longlining involves a long main line with baited hooks attached at branch-like intervals.
2. Total allowable catch is the total amount of fish that can be caught sustainably each year. Countries set these limits based on advice from fisheries scientists.

Transnational Fishers' Movements

Birth, Consolidation, Evolution and Contestation

In the face of the exclusionary development and structural transformations that have occurred in fisheries globally, fishers and fishing communities have been forced to adapt or find ways to challenge and resist the continuously emerging obstacles. As the previous chapter argues, structural transformations have emerged from the combined consequences of the industrialization, privatization and conservation waves in global fisheries, which have benefitted large-scale industrial companies while excluding and threatening the survival of small-scale fishers. The establishment of social movements has been a key strategy for mobilization and collectively amplifying fishers' voices. Tracking the historical evolution of transnational movements sheds light on the particularities and significance of the role these movements play in the politics of global fisheries. This chapter explores how transnational fishers' movements have evolved over the last three decades and their political agendas and strategies. It delves into the political developments which contributed to the emergence of the movements in the 1980s and 90s and why and how they have built transnational alliances with agrarian movements and intergovernmental organizations.

Building an International Fishers' Network

The narrative that is woven together in this chapter provides a historical account of transnational fishers' movements, pieced together through archival document collection, conversations, interviews and participant observation. Considering that history is told and understood differently by different actors based on their subjectivity and experiences, this historical account likely leaves out some moments or interactions which others may see as important. Therefore, the history offered here is not presented as the definitive story of the transnational fishers' movements but is rather a story that has been carefully assembled and woven together to develop a narrative. Not all the fascinating stories that I collected throughout the research process could be included in this book. I had to make choices about what and what not to include in order to offer coherence and direction and make connections with the arguments I present in this book. What unfolds is a story of two transnational movements representing small-scale fishers, the World Forum of Fish Harvesters and Fish Workers (WFF) and the World Forum of Fisher Peoples (WFFP) — which began as one and later split into two — and the events leading up to and emerging from their establishment.

The 1984 Conference

The story begins in Rome in July 1984 at the International Conference of Fishworkers and Their Supporters, which became a famous first step toward establishing a transnational movement.[1] In many of the interviews I conducted with movement members and supporters who have been involved since the early 1980s, the "1984 Conference," as it is often referred to, was noted as the space where it all began (see also WFF, 2000). The 1984 Conference was conceived as a first step toward building solidarity between fishers' organizations from around the world, particularly the Global South. It was self-organized by fishers' organizations and supporters working with fishing communities and involved 100 participants from 34 countries, including 50 fishworkers (small-scale fishers, fishing crew workers, processers and sellers) and 50 supporters (individuals and representatives of organizations working with fishworkers) from Africa, Asia, Europe, Latin America, North America and Oceania. The conference report notes that it was a historical event since fishworkers had previously been excluded from discussions and decision-making processes at both the project level and the broader policy level (Cooperation of People, 1984; Kurien, 2007; 1996). The report, which was written by a group of the organizers calling themselves the Cooperation of People in Asia, Latin America and Africa, explains:

> At this conference they [fishworkers] decided to initiate a process of building international collaboration and solidarity. This process will enable them to overcome the barriers to shaping their own future. It was a people's initiative. Not waiting for an international governmental bodies' invitation, they decided to meet on

> their own initiative, with their own style, own agenda and own working methods. This conference was not conceived as an intellectual experience. It became a living human experience in which spontaneity, life-sharing and self-expression at all levels played a major role. It was a committed encounter. It carried an emotional meaning and an existential weight which added to its seriousness. It was a direct result of the fact that the participants live through the problems which they discuss and hence become dramatically concerned with solutions. It was a state in an ongoing process of struggles and collective action. Rooted in direct experience at local level, this was an attempt to relate beyond national and regional boundaries. (Cooperation of People, 1984, 5)

The aim of the conference was to share concrete life experiences; gain insights into the problems faced by fishers' organizations and the solutions they proposed; reach a better understanding of political and economic mechanisms operating at the global level; develop alternatives that ensure the reappropriation of the sea and the future survival of fishworkers; and devise ways to build up national, regional and international solidarity and coordinate activities. The conference proceedings included country reports by participants; plenary sessions and collective discussions on key issues; inter-regional group meetings; audio-visual displays on participant concerns; an exhibition of newsletters, photographs, pedagogical materials

International Conference of Fishworkers and their supporters (Rome). Source: ICSF, 1984.

and models of fishing crafts expressing people's experiences and struggles; a field visit to an Italian fishing cooperative; and a demonstration of song, dance and storytelling in the centre of Rome (Cooperation of People, 1984; Kurien, 2007; 1996).

While much of the money for the conference came from fundraising by the participating organizations, some participants, who had also joined the FAO World Conference on Fisheries Management and Development a few days prior, were able to access travel funds from FAO. The FAO conference, which focused on developing an international strategy for fisheries management and development, included 147 national delegates, 62 fisheries ministers, representatives from 14 United Nations bodies and 3 African liberation movements, and observers from 24 intergovernmental organizations and 29 international NGOs (FAO, 1984; Kurien, 2007). Rolf Willmann, a German economist who joined FAO's Rome-based Fisheries Division in 1982 to prepare for the 1984 events, played an active role in both conferences. During his thirty-year career at FAO, he proved to be a crucial ally for fishers' organizations and movements in gaining access to formal FAO spaces (FAO, 2013). One interviewee from a civil society organization explained:

> Rolf would host us [during meetings] in Rome. We were all in negotiations together during the day, and then in the evening we'd meet him to continue discussions over dinner. He was genuinely committed to supporting the fishers and fishworker movement. There was this feeling that we're all in this together. Especially in the early days of developing submissions that later fed into the SSF Guidelines,[2] it was always "well let's check with Rolf to see what he thinks" and to see if the wording we were using would float with FAO.

The participants in the 1984 Conference established two overarching conclusions: first, despite geographical, political, social and economic differences at the national level, common factors cause the same problems in fisheries globally. They recognized that national boundaries and polarization between Global South and Global North interests must be overcome and that "unless the problems are analysed in the framework of a world capitalist system which integrates the economic sectors of all countries, no effective solution can be found to improve the predicament of fishworkers" (Cooperation of People, 1984, 8). Second, although numerous positive lessons can be drawn from country-level experiences, workers' organizations and collective actions must acknowledge the concrete socio-political context that they operate within. The crucial outcome of the conference was to begin building up a solidarity network of national-level fishers' organizations by directing efforts toward creating a solid mass-based organization. This included facilitating communication between sub-regional groups of fishers, establishing the Coordination Committee of regional network representatives and taking steps to ensure that small-scale fishers' organizations got representative status in ILO (Cooperation of People, 1984; Kurien, 2007).

International Collective in Support of Fishworkers (1986)

Two years later, the sparks that were ignited at the 1984 Conference contributed to the establishment of the International Collective in Support of Fishworkers (ICSF) by many of the supporters who participated in and helped organize the conference. This was a second crucial step toward establishing a transnational movement. ICSF, a long-standing support organization of the transnational fishers' movements, was officially established at the 1986 International Workshop on Issues in Fisheries Development: Towards an International Collective in Support of Fishworkers, held in Trivandrum, India. This workshop, which was organized and hosted by the South Indian Federation of Fishermen Societies and the Centre for

Demonstration in the centre of Rome during the 1984 Conference. Source: ICSF, 1984.

Development Studies, brought together 40 participants from 18 countries, including activists, social scientists, marine biologists, economists and engineers who worked with fishers and traditional fisheries. The aim of the workshop was to review the outcomes of and organize concrete follow-up to the 1984 Conference. The participants concluded that an official collective would be established, based on informal contact between its members and in which trust, understanding and good working relationships were key. The collective would not claim to represent fishers but would be a group of individuals committed to supporting them, focused on tackling issues at the international level and maintaining critical working relationships with technical assistance agencies (such as FAO) on a consultative basis. This marked the beginning of ICSF, which more than three decades later still plays a crucial role in providing research, technical and project support to the transnational fishers' movements in numerous political spaces and processes (ICSF, 1986; WFF, 2000).

ICSF is an international NGO, which draws its mandate from the 1984 Conference, supporting, collaborating with and empowering fishing communities and organizations and working toward establishing "equitable, gender-just, self-reliant and sustainable fisheries, particularly in the small-scale artisanal sector" (ICSF, 2021). As a support organization, ICSF focuses on influencing national, regional and international decision-making pro-

International Workshop on Issues in Fisheries Development (Trivandrum). Source: ICSF, 1986.

cesses in fisheries, underlining the importance of small-scale fisheries and fishing communities. Its structure includes an elected board, which steers the agenda and programs, a general assembly of members, which contributes to and takes decisions on campaigns and activities and a secretariat, which handles program coordination, organizational functions and administration.

ICSF and its members are propelled by a vision in which fishers and fishing communities live a dignified life, where their rights and livelihoods are protected and they are organized in a way that supports the democratic, equitable, sustainable and responsible use of natural resources. Its main aims are to monitor issues related to the lives, livelihoods and living conditions of fishworkers around the world; disseminate information on these issues, particularly to fishers; prepare policy guidelines focusing on just, participatory and sustainable fisheries development and management; and help create space and momentum to develop alternatives in the small-scale fisheries sector (ICSF, 2021). ICSF has played a crucial role in fostering collaboration between transnational fishers' movements and the FAO Fisheries Division; building partnerships between the movements and research and technical institutions through involvement in projects; and contributing to the development and endorsement of the Small-Scale Fisheries Guidelines. A few interviewees noted that without the support of ICSF, the fishers' movements may not have had the capacity to analyze and engage with complex fisheries politics and processes or gain access to important FAO spaces, such as the Committee on Fisheries (COFI), which is discussed in detail in Chapter 4.

Quebec City Meeting and Anti-WTO Protests (1995)

A little over a decade after the 1984 Conference and the establishment of ICSF, a third crucial step in the construction of a transnational fishers' movement took place. During a meeting of fishers' organizations from Africa, Asia, North America and Latin America in Quebec City, Canada, in October 1995, a decision was made to organize the World Forum of Fish Harvesters and Fishworkers. This decision emerged out of the recognition that fishing was largely absent from the agenda of the FAO Symposium on World Food Security, which fishers' organizations were attending in Quebec at the time. The founding of the World Trade Organization (WTO)in January of that year and the increasing neoliberal globalization of fish trade were also pinpointed as central threats to small-scale fisheries. The fisher representatives that were present at the FAO Symposium agreed that the discussions that were taking place at the international level about issues such as exploitation of fishworkers, threats to sustainability and management of fisheries resources were meaningless without fisher participation. They recognized that, in order to propose alternatives that would protect small-scale fishers' livelihoods and ways of life, this participation could only be made possible through political organization at the international level and representation in a global forum of fisher peoples (WFF, 1997, 2000).

The unfolding process of neoliberal globalization, which had begun in the 1970s and continued to escalate, leading to the founding of the WTO in 1995, was a crucial catalyst in the emergence of transnational movements of small-scale food producers, like WFF and LVC (Smith, 2013). Gaventa and Tandon note:

> With globalization have come changing forms of power and new realms of authority, and with these, new spaces for public action. From local to global, fields of power and landscapes of authority are being reconfigured, affecting the lives and futures of citizens across the planet, while simultaneously reshaping where and how citizens engage to make their voices heard. (2010, 3)

WTO and the neoliberal policies it promoted further intensified the international trade of food to the benefit of large-scale industrial fishing and agriculture companies with the economic capacity and motivation to expand their markets. This system poses a direct threat to small-scale fishers and farmers, who do not have the same capacities, nor do they — in many cases — have an interest in selling their products internationally. In response to the corporate takeover of the global food system, many small-scale producers who were challenging the predominant neoliberal model of globalization decided to link their struggles and form transnational movements like LVC (in 1993) and WFF (in 1997) (Edelman and Borras, 2016; Levkoe, 2014; Smith, 2013). Certainly, those who established these movements were connected in various ways through global justice work since well before the 1990s, steadily building up networks in an era without internet and cell phones, using fax machines and landlines to connect internationally. This seems like a nearly impossible feat, especially reflecting on this from a time when WhatsApp conversations, emails and Zoom calls are part of our daily routines and communication within social movements is still riddled with challenges. Yet, the developments of the 1990s, particularly protests that erupted over the founding of WTO and subsequent ministerial negotiations, contributed to a significant scaling up of transnational activism (Smith, 2013). The activists who were present at the Quebec City fishers' meeting

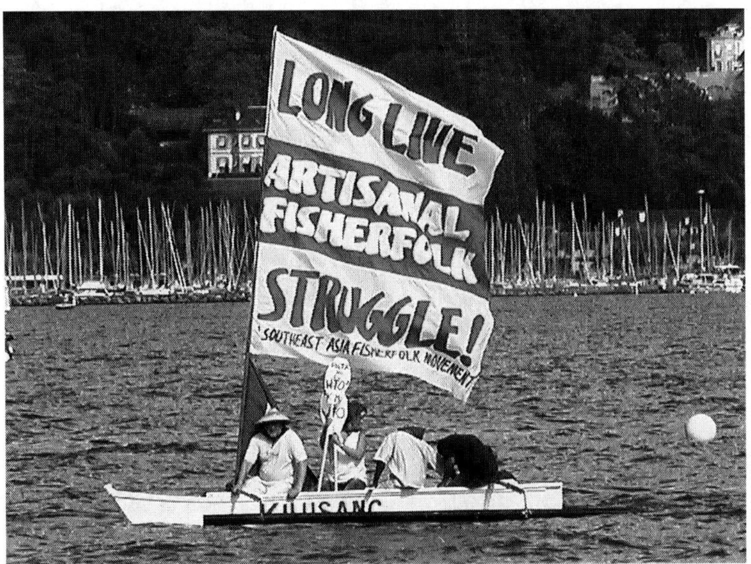

Fishers protest against the establishment of the WTO (Geneva). Source: Johnston, 1995.

in 1995 and went on to form WFF two years later were also deeply involved in the anti-WTO protests, even organizing a dramatic boat protest in Lake Geneva in the summer of 1995.

Birth of the World Fishers' Forum (1997)

The World Forum, also known as the 1st WFF General Assembly, was organized in November 1997 in New Delhi and hosted by the National Fishworkers Forum (NFF) of India. November 21 was also the celebration of the first World Fisheries Day, an event focusing on the crucial contributions of fishers and fishing communities, which continues to be celebrated annually. The aim was to bring together fish harvesters and fishworkers from around the world to discuss "how to preserve the world's fish resources through an appropriate conservation and management regime, which includes the regulated common property rights of coastal communities to the coastal sea and its resources" (WFF, 1997, 5). With 150 fisher delegates from 32 countries and 126 observers and advisors participating in the Forum, this would be the first time that fishers' organizations from the Global North and South would come together en masse to develop a strategy for tackling the global fisheries crisis (Johnston, 1997).

Four Main Objectives of the 1st WFF General Assembly

1) To continue the discussion on sustainable fishing among fish harvester and fishworker organizations that began in Quebec City;
2) To work towards the formulation of a resource management regime that incorporates the common property rights of coastal communities to the coastal sea and its resources;
3) To work to halt the worldwide depletion of fish stocks by industrial fleets; and
4) To develop a worldwide solidarity organization of fish harvesters and fish-workers as a natural corollary to the globalization of exploitation, in order to propose alternatives that would preserve and nurture the fish resources and the fishing communities that depend on them for their livelihood. (WFF, 1997, 6)

Andy Johnston, a South African fisher from the Artisanal Fishers Association and founding member of the WFF, noted:

> Discussions at the conference centred around the need, structure and membership of the proposed WFF. The wide diversity in the contexts of the different fishworker organizations led to differing perceptions on many of these questions, but considerable progress was made in identifying the issues and at working out the options. The delegates eventually reached an understanding on the formation of a new world body to represent their interests at the international level, after much debate and discussion. Given the great differences between countries, it was plain that it required an organization of great flexibility to accommodate the fishers and their organizations from all over the world. (Johnston, 1997)

By the end of the meeting, WFF was officially inaugurated, the Charter was drafted, including an organizational structure, and the interim Steering Committee and head coordinator were elected to guide the process. The elected coordinator was Thomas Kocherry, an Indian activist and priest who was a prominent leader in fishing communities in India and also chair of NFF at the time (WFF, 1997; Sall et al., 2002). The Steering Committee, which would later become the larger Coordination Committee (CC), would be responsible for carrying out all regular coordinating duties of an international organization; facilitating the formation of regional councils; drafting a constitution, including guidelines for certification of voting and non-voting membership; and holding a constituent assembly (including all WFF members) within three years of the 1st General Assembly. The future structure of WFF was also proposed, which included the General Assembly,

First World Forum of Fish Harvesters and Fishworkers General Assembly. (New Delhi) Source: Johnston, 1997.

involving all member organizations, and the CC, formed through regional representation. The CC would include one male and one female representative from each of the five participating regions (Africa, Asia, Europe, North America and Latin America) in order to ensure gender balance. Members from each region could also create councils for coordination and consultation at the regional level, but their membership would be directly in WFF and not in the regional council (WFF, 1997; WFF, 2000).

Charter of 14 Objectives for WFF's Work

(proposed by the Steering Committee)

1) Protect and enhance the coastal communities that depend on the fishery for their livelihood.
2) Create an understanding of the resources as a collective heritage and ensure, through sustainable fishing, conservation and regeneration of the resources and the marine ecosystem, that it is passed on to future generations.
3) Protect fishing communities and fish resources from both land-based and sea-based threats (for example, displacement by tourism, pollution, aquaculture, overfishing and destructive fishing practices).
4) Maintain and promote a regime that will ensure the traditional and customary rights of coastal communities to the fishery.
5) Promote the primary role of fish harvesters' and fishworkers' organizations in managing fisheries and oceans, nationally and internationally.

6) Ensure food security both locally and worldwide through sustaining stocks for the future.
7) Represent fish harvesters and fishworkers in all appropriate international and regional fora and advocate for their recognition in such organizations (for example, ILO, FAO, UN).
8) Serve as a watchdog to ensure compliance by states with international agreements and to prevent the export of the fishery crisis and of technologies that lead to this crisis.
9) Provide mutual support for national and international struggles.
10) Encourage fish harvesters and fishworkers to organize where such organizations do not exist.
11) Recognize, preserve and enhance the role of women in the fishing economy and in the sustenance of the community.
12) Secure and develop the economic viability and quality of life of fish harvesters, fishworkers and their communities.
13) Preserve and enhance the unique culture of fishing communities.
14) Affirm a culture of the sea as mother and source of life. (WFF, 1997, 61–62)

The initial intention of WFF was to be registered as an international organization; however, during the 1st General Assembly some participants felt that organizational status would make membership too strict. The Acts of WFF (1997) state that WFF members include organizations such as trade unions, associations, federations of democratically constituted cooperatives and Indigenous Nations dependent upon the fishery for their livelihood. There should preferably only be one member organization per country, and if there are more than one, organizations seeking membership should be able to prove that they are representative of the majority of the constituencies listed above (WFF, 1997). The terminology used in the membership rules became problematic, with terms like fishworker, owner/operator, artisanal, Indigenous and traditional implying different meanings in the context of different national fisheries (Johnston, 1997). Interestingly, during the General Assembly, several members suggested that instead of an organization, it would be better for WFF to be considered a movement in order for membership criteria to be broader and more inclusive. This would allow the membership criteria to simply state that members must be legitimate fishers' organizations that agree with WFF objectives and are approved by the regional review committees (WFF, 1997, 2000). This debate about the organizational-versus-movement status of WFF, membership criteria (who is in and who is out) and the politics surrounding these issues were important signals of internal friction bubbling up within the movement. This friction ended up being an important precursor for the later political divisions and organizational split that would transpire three years later at the 2nd General Assembly, in Loctudy, France.

In the three years following the 1st General Assembly in New Delhi, WFF worked toward building its network and strengthening coordination, communication and connections between member organizations. The interim Steering Committee shifted into the CC, as planned in the organizational structure (see Figure 3.1) and held its second and third meetings in Namur, Belgium, in October 1998, and in San Francisco, United States, in October 1999. The aim of these meetings was for the CC to finalize the logistical and administrative requirements of establishing an international organization, including the structure, as well as to draft the constitution and the various policies. During discussions about the constitution in San Francisco, the CC agreed that membership would be simplified to "independent owner-operators" and that WFF objectives would be finalized as follows:

> To protect fishing communities, fish resources and fish habitats, such as coastal zones, watersheds, and mangroves, from both land-based and sea-based threats. These include displacement by tourism, pollution (including the use of the sea as a dumping ground for toxic waste), destructive industrial aquaculture, overfishing and destructive fishing practices. (WFF, 1999, 3)

Figure 3.1 WFF Organizational Structure

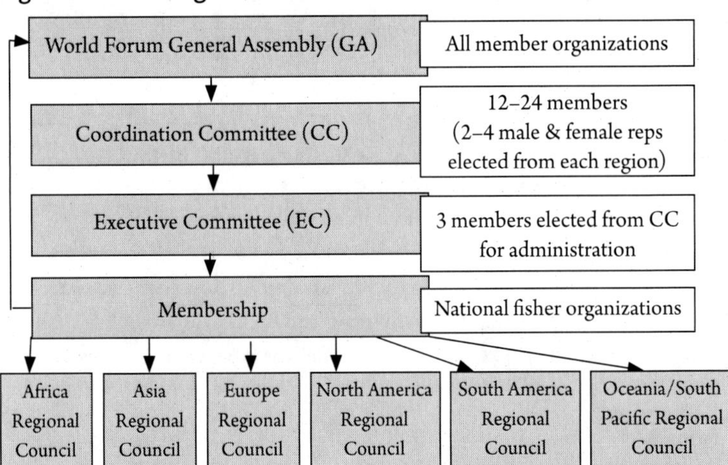

Source: author (using WFF 1997, 1999 information).

The CC was designated as the only body that could admit new active members, as well as suspend or expel members (through a two-thirds vote) for non-payment of fees or actions deemed detrimental to the objectives of WFF. During the San Francisco meeting, it was decided that the next CC meeting would be in April 2000, in Loctudy, France, in preparation for the 2nd WFF General Assembly, which would also be held in Loctudy in October (WFF, 1999, 2000).

Internal Splits and New Beginnings in Loctudy (2000)

Following two years of extensive and complicated preparations, 200 delegates from 34 countries came together in October 2000 for the 2nd General Assembly. The French WFF members, who were hosting the meeting in Loctudy — a small fishing village with only a few thousand inhabitants in southwestern France — worked hard to ensure that every detail had been attended to, including soliciting support from the French authorities and the European Union. The participating delegates included a broad spectrum of fisheries actors, such as national fishers' organizations and committees, large- and small-scale fishers from the Atlantic and Mediterranean coasts and women's groups. While the assembly began relatively smoothly and constructively, three days in, tensions began to bubble over among the members (O'Riordan, 2000).

There are many different perspectives on the details of what transpired during the infamous Loctudy meeting. Written accounts and the people I interviewed — some of whom participated in the assembly, while others recounted secondhand stories about the event — reflected on slightly different aspects of what happened. Yet, the result was that half of the WFF members walked out of the meeting to form a second movement — the WFFP. A common theme in many accounts of the split was that the there was a clash between members from Europe and North America (particularly Canada) and those from Africa and Asia (particularly India) about how the organization should operate and the criteria for membership. One big point of contention was what is considered "small-scale fisheries" in the North and South in terms of boat size and gear and methods used, with some southern members accusing northern members of being too commercialized to understand the struggles of a real fishworker. A fieldtrip to a French fishing community sparked heated debate when some of the Indian members commented on the large scale of France's small-scale fisheries (see also Sall et al.). One of the Canadian WFF members from the Maritime Fishermen's Union (MFU), Michael Belliveau, who passed away in 2002, not long after the Loctudy meeting, wrote:

> The World Forum was the first attempt ever of small-scale fishermen and fishworkers to formally associate at the global level. After four days of debate and workshops directed to adopting a constitution, half the delegates walked out to form a second forum. The leader of the walkout is said to have stated that the split was inevitable and that he was satisfied to be free from the "harvesters" to get on with his "fishworker" concerns. An MFU type of organization is an easy mark for persons who build their fight around identity or race or numbers. Our members could be termed "harvesters," although I always knew them as inshore fishermen… Most of the crew members on our inshore boats are not in the MFU… the Afro-Asian bloc that walked out at Loctudy appeared to be oblivious to the nature of our type of organization. (Sall et al., 2002, 164)

A South African member I interviewed, who had participated in the assembly and joined the newly formed WFFP, noted:

> We from the South, and they from the North, had a difference of opinion. There are two things I realize now: One, it was a power struggle, people didn't want to give up positions. And secondly, it was a different ideology completely. There were NGOs and there were fisherfolks. And those from the East had a bit of a problem with NGOs, so that came to the fore, and then there was a split.

In another account, Brian O'Riordan, a long-time ICSF member from the United Kingdom who was also present at the assembly, wrote:

> On Thursday afternoon, as the Indians and Canadians struggled to wrest control of the WFF, heated and emotional exchanges ensued. This culminated in a bizarre debate over the number of continents, following which voting took place. As the tide turned against the Indians, chaos ensued, and half of the assembly walked out. Unity was on the rocks. (2000, 4)

In a response to O'Riordan's article, Savarimuthu Santiago, a former member of the WFF Secretariat and subsequently of the newly formed WFFP Secretariat, wrote:

> A few facts amply demonstrate that while the lobby led by the Canadian delegation struggled for power, the lobby led by the

> Indian delegation was forced to join the struggle, not to wield power, but for freedom, equality and survival. (2001, 1)

The common thread running through the accounts was that the split was caused by internal power struggles and differences of opinion over how the organization should be structured and led. This was largely the result of ideological, personal and political tensions that exist within all social organizations and movements, whether they be at the local, national or transnational level. The dynamics that exist within transnational movements are particularly complex due to the diversity of the membership within these groups in terms of national, political, economic, social, cultural and ethnic backgrounds. While transnational movements typically require a high level of cohesion, shared collective identity and regular horizontal communication between members, a strong feeling of connection is often difficult to maintain (Fox, 2010). This becomes even more of a challenge when there is little direct contact between members aside from a triennial general assembly and occasional meetings for coordination or international events which do not involve all members. Many of the people I interviewed noted how crucial it is for movement members to regularly meet in person in order to build up trust and rapport; otherwise, relationships can quickly become strained. Reflecting on some of the catalysts of the split, Table 3.1 details some of the challenges WFF faced in its first three years.

Delegates walk out of the 2nd WFF General Assembly to form WFFP (Loctudy). Source: Johnston, 2000.

Table 3.1: Challenges to Unity in WFF (1997–2000)

Characteristics	Transnational Movements	WFF
Exchange of information and experiences	Shared	Occurred mainly through a triennial general assembly and occasional meetings for coordination and international events, which do not involve all members. Otherwise dependent on telephone and fax communication, which many members did not have regular access to. Substantial exchanges became infrequent and difficult.
Organized social base	Counterparts have bases	Some member organizations were much stronger, more vocal and more mobilized than others, which can cause an imbalance in perspectives contributing to agenda-setting and political direction. Members also came from very different contexts and approaches to organization, which can conflict.
Mutual support	Shared	Members need to feel a sense of support from each other and that they have shared struggles that bind them together. Solidarity actions addressing national issues are also important, and without this, members may not see the value of their participation in a transnational movement. In the pre-internet era, communication around international solidarity was much more difficult. Access to international news was also much more limited.
Material interests	Sometimes shared	While many members faced similar issues of exclusion and marginalization in the fisheries sector, on the surface there was a noticeable difference between the material conditions of fishers from the North and South. This was reflected in the debates around who should be considered a small-scale fisher and membership criteria.
Joint actions and campaigns	Shared, based on shared long-term strategy	Many members participated in joint actions prior to 1997, with a lot of energy put into the anti-WTO protests. However, in the early years of WFF there had not yet been a clear strategy or campaigns established, which meant that members may not have found enough common activities to collaborate on and build connections within the movement.

Characteristics	Transnational Movements	WFF
Ideologies	Usually shared	Members engage in diverse approaches to fishing, have different roles in their national fisheries contexts and different economic positions, so ideologies also differed in how to challenge the dominant neoliberal model. Some members had a more radical agenda to directly challenge the capitalist system, while others were embedded in the system and focused on ways to improve their position. This presented a crucial obstacle to agenda-setting within the movement.
Collective identities and political cultures	Shared political values, repertoires and identities	Members came from very different political, social, economic, ethnic and cultural backgrounds, which impacted the ability to develop a collective identity and values. Developing a shared identity is a complicated and long process which can take years of internal discussion.

Source: author (expanded from Fox's 2010 typology on characteristics of transnational movements).

Thus, in a "movement of movements," such as WFF, which is constituted of many national fishers' organizations, group dynamics are bound to be fraught. When analyzing what transpired at the Loctudy meeting, one cannot help but wonder whether things could have been worked out over time if some delegates had not decided to leave WFF and form a second movement. Perhaps members could have found more common ground and ideological synergy if there had been more willingness to discuss fundamental internal issues and find a compromise. Personal tensions and leadership dynamics also played an important role, particularly considering there were several very strong leaders in WFF, such as Kocherry, a priest who had powerful public-speaking and mobilization skills. Several interviewees commented that the leaders on both sides of the split were dominant men coming from strong organizations who were used to working in a certain way and not having to share power. Transnational agrarian movements have also historically had largely or entirely male leadership (Edelman and Borras, 2016). In the fishers' movement, these leaders had decades of experience mobilizing fishers at the national level, were extremely skilled at building solidarity within a familiar social and political context and were being confronted with the complications of building a movement with a diverse group from very different contexts. These factors certainly played a role in how the conflict unfolded and why some members felt that the split was inevitable (see also Sall et al., 2002).

Thomas Kocherry, WFF coordinator, addressing the General Assembly (Loctudy). Source: Johnston, 2000.

Regardless of which perspective is the most accurate in terms of who said or did what, the outcome was the same: WFF split in half, with the formation of a second transnational movement, WFFP. While the North and South American, Icelandic and French members chose to remain in WFF, the newly formed WFFP included members from Africa, Asia, New Zealand, Spain and a Canadian First Nations community (Sinha, 2012). Reflecting on this outcome, O'Riordan raises an important point about the similarity of the principles both movements maintained:

> People are struggling to understand what happened and why. Did it mean that work on building global unity and solidarity amongst fishing communities had to start again from scratch? Had this set back more than 15 years of work (since Rome in 1984)? Who and what were to blame? Such questions will, and can, never be answered. They may even be counterproductive, hiding a basic reality. True, a division had occurred, but apart from the French and others who had invested so much time and effort, and apart from anger, hurt feelings and pride, what were the real casualties? While some had chosen to remain on the WFF boat, the new vessel that emerged was founded on the same basic principles that had launched the venture in the first place. (2000, 4)

WFF and WFFP have maintained important commonalities in the overarching issues they focus on, such as fishers' human rights and encroachment on small-scale fishing areas. In both movements' constitutions, the commitment to challenging the dominant model of industrial development, globalized markets and concentration of ownership over fisheries resources and property in the hands of the powerful also remain (O'Riordan, 2000). These commonalities are arguably the main reason why these movements have continued to collaborate, particularly since 2012, when WFF re-emerged after a period of relative inactivity and many of the people who had been centrally involved in the split had either passed away or were no longer active in the movements. This collaboration is discussed in more detail later in this chapter.

The two movements have also had different historical trajectories, evolving somewhat differently in terms of their political character, level of mobilization and activities. As mentioned earlier, important tensions had emerged between those who believed WFF should be registered as an international organization — which would offer more political legitimacy and access to external funding — and those who regarded it as a social movement — which would allow more autonomy and flexibility. Many of those who joined WFFP had called for the latter option, an ideology still evident in the movement. In terms of membership, public lists show that WFF currently has 44 member organizations (WFF, 2020b), while WFFP has 75 (WFFP, 2020b) (see Table 3.2). Yet, as one WFFP interviewee noted, "In many countries, even today, we have dual membership." Interestingly, both movements' constitutions (see WFF, 2020c; WFFP, 2020c) list the same criteria for membership, which reflects the fact that their constitutions have remained largely similar since the split (O'Riordan, 2000).

WFF's and WFFP's Membership Criteria

1) Fish harvesters (including subsistence, artisanal and traditional coastal and inland fishers; aboriginal or indigenous peoples who are customary fish harvesters; independent small-scale owner-operators; crew members in this sector);
2) Crew members of fishing units other than those mentioned above;
3) Broadly based (mass-based) organizations of fishing communities and women engaged in work in support of the fishery;
4) Fish workers who are engaged in activities related to the processing, direct sale (excluding merchants) or transport of fish. (Source: WFF, 2020c; WFFP, 2020c).

Table 3.2: WFF and WFFP Member Organizations and Countries (2020)

WFF	WFFP
Total Member Organizations: 44 Countries: 41 Africa (16): Algeria, Burundi, Chad, Djibouti, Gambia, Ghana, Guinea, Kenya, Mauritania, Morocco, Nigeria, Sierra Leone, Tunisia, Uganda, Tanzania, Somalia Asia (2): China, India Europe (6): Greenland, Faroe Islands, Iceland, Norway, Portugal, France North America (3): Canada, Mexico, United States Latin America (14): Belize, Dominican Republic, Argentina, Brazil, Chile, Costa Rica, Ecuador, El Salvador, Guatemala, Honduras, Nicaragua, Panama, Peru, Venezuela	Total Member Organizations: 75 Countries: 47 Africa (16): Benin, Gambia, Guinea, Kenya, Madagascar, Mali, Martinique, Mauritania, Mauritius, Reunion, Seychelles, Senegal, Sierra Leone, South Africa, Uganda, DR Congo Asia (10): Bangladesh, India, Indonesia, Malaysia, Pakistan, Philippines, Sri Lanka, Thailand, Palestine, Turkey Europe (3): Spain, France, Russia North America (1): Canada Oceania (1): New Zealand Latin America and the Caribbean (16): Guadeloupe, Honduras, Jamaica, Antigua and Barbuda, Bahamas, Barbados, Belize, Dominica, Grenada, St. Kitts and Nevis, St. Lucia, St. Vincent, Suriname, Trinidad and Tobago, Ecuador, Brazil

Source: author (using WFF 2020b and WFFP 2020b information).

Evolution of Two Transnational Movements

In the years following the split, WFF and WFFP went through their own processes of growth, developing distinct advocacy strategies and approaches to collaboration and resistance. In an interview, a WFFP member described the following four distinct periods of growth for the global movement, in which certain characteristics and challenges can be identified:

1) 2000 to 2004, before the Indian Ocean earthquake and tsunami occurred;
2) 2005 to 2008, when the Global Conference on Small-Scale Fisheries took place in Bangkok;
3) 2009 to 2014, Small-Scale Fisheries Guidelines negotiations and endorsement; and
4) 2014 to 2020, post-Guidelines endorsement.

A WFFP member explained that, in the early 2000s, WFFP's focus was on internal capacity-building and planning meetings. Everything was centred around when the Coordination Committee (CC) meeting and General Assembly were going to be held. In each General Assembly, preparations would already begin for the next two CC meetings and next General Assembly, and if there happened to be a COFI session in between, then participation in that also had to be planned.

In 2001, the WFFP CC held its first meeting in Mumbai, India. The main aim of the meeting was to develop a concrete plan of action for the next three years of WFFP's international work and establish ways to carry it out. The opening paragraphs of the meeting report state that the first general body meeting of WFFP, which took place in Loctudy after the split, "had unanimously accepted a new constitution," in which they excluded "corporations, transnational companies and allied affiliates owning fishing vessels and engaged in harvesting, processing and distribution of fish and those carrying out destructive fishing or industrial aquaculture" from joining the movement (WFFP, 2001, 3). The report also points out that, while it was an important achievement for WFFP as a young organization to have

WFFP CC Meeting in Sri Lanka (Nainamadama). Source: Johnston, 2003.

already become visible at the international level, it still had "miles more to go in building up international fish workers solidarity and also to devise effective means of resistance to the rapid economic changes happening in the name of globalization and open markets" (5). The report notes that another major decision that was taken in Loctudy was to continue to observe World Fisheries Day on November 21 each year as a day "to establish the right of fishing communities to own water bodies, fishing implements and to manage the distribution of their catch" (4). The annual celebration of World Fisheries Day, which is another commonality between WFF and WFFP, continues to serve as a unifying event.

Indian Ocean Earthquake and Tsunami (2004)

The period between 2000 and 2004 was the first distinct phase in WFFP's history, in which its strength was largely situated in Asia, particularly among movement leaders in India, Pakistan and Sri Lanka who had long-standing experience organizing fishers nationally. This first phase ended abruptly due to the disastrous aftermath of the December 2004 Indian Ocean earthquake and tsunami, which killed more than 225,000 people. The vast majority of those effected by this disaster were coastal and fishing communities in Sri Lanka, India, Thailand, Malaysia and Indonesia (see Ahmadun et al., 2020; De Silva and Yamao, 2007), some of which WFFP members were part of or worked with. Reflecting on the tsunami, one member told me that the aftermath of this disaster changed the life and character of the movement:

> The leadership that we had in WFFP from the late 1990s stood through until 2004. It was the same kind of people to a large degree, very little new thinking, very little new people other than those who were there when it all started. So they did things pretty much the same way. But when the tsunami hit, it impacted quite hard on WFFP... The impact it had on WFFP activists outside of the tsunami areas was great because the consciousness was there, the ideology was there, the solidarity was there, but the organization wasn't there. So, the first thing that people were inclined to do was say there are hundreds of fishing communities under severe stress, we've got to find a way to help.

WFFP activists came up with three ways to help, including sending money to aid recovery and burial processes; contributing to rehabilitation in fishing communities that had been destroyed; and rebuilding fishing vessels and fisheries. An interviewee revealed that this triggered a sense of organization:

> It was organization around support, organization around solidarity, nationally in India, Sri Lanka and Asia in general, but also globally, because WFFP had existed but not that efficiently or effectively as a global network, but certainly present. The first thing that people like Tom Kocherry and Harekrishna [Indian WFFP leaders at the time] would do was to send out messages to allies, friends and contacts across the world. And that brought all the WFFP people together; it gave a sense of purpose globally, of belonging to a solidarity movement, because this was something that we could do… The tsunami, as bad as it was, triggered a new energy in the WFFP movement. It was an important moment.

Bangkok Conference and Statement (2008)

In the post-tsunami period between 2004 and 2008, solidarity and mobilization continued to grow in the fishers' movements, and the network expanded. A second distinct phase began in 2008, when FAO and the Thai government organized the Global Conference on Small-Scale Fisheries in Bangkok in response to a request from the 27th COFI Session in 2007. The conference focused on developing a strategy for securing sustainable small-scale fisheries by bringing together responsible fisheries and social development. More than 280 participants from 65 countries attended the conference, including fisheries managers, fishworkers, scientists, government officials and representatives from professional associations, NGOs, civil society and the private sector. The format centred around presentations, panel statements and working group discussions covering a wide range of issues, including social and economic development, human rights, fisheries management, governance and policy processes and access to post-harvest markets. Special emphasis was placed on securing access and user rights to coastal and inland fisheries resources for small-scale fisheries, fishing communities and Indigenous Peoples (FAO, 2008).

A few days prior to the conference, WFFP, in collaboration with ICSF and several Thai civil society organizations (CSOs), organized a civil society workshop and the WFFP CC meeting. When they were unable to find a venue to host the CC meeting, a local fisher offered the hull of his boat. One WFFP member recalled this meeting with a laugh:

> So we went over to his boat, and there were about 50 of us crammed into this sort of enclosed boat, but it was the only space that we could be together and speak and meet. I remember that moment so, so clearly. Not all of us could even fit in because it was

> just way too small. And we battled with interpretation because we had no interpreters with us there, just a few people who were able to do it on the side.

However haphazard this meeting felt at the time, it would turn out to be one of the most important in WFFP's history. It was in that meeting that the Bangkok Statement was drafted, in which the global demands of small-scale fishing communities were set out. Several interviewees mentioned that the Statement was extremely important for making WFFP's demands visible at the international level, particularly within FAO (see also Pictou, 2015). The Statement, a collaboration between 106 representatives from small-scale fishing and Indigenous communities and their supporters from 36 countries, notes that it builds upon prior preparatory processes and workshops organized by WFFP, ICSF and allied organizations in Asia, Africa and Latin America. The Statement presents 36 demands, calling upon FAO and other UN agencies, regional fisheries bodies and national governments to secure the access rights, post-harvest rights and human rights of small-scale fishers. The opening of the Statement declares:

> Recognizing the principle of food sovereignty outlined in the Nyelini Declaration. Declaring that the human rights of fishing

Participants at the WFFP CC Meeting in Bangkok. Source: Johnston, 2008.

> communities are indivisible and that the development of responsible and sustainable small-scale and indigenous fisheries is possible only if their political, civil, social, economic and cultural rights are addressed in an integrated manner. Recognizing that all rights and freedoms apply equally to all men and women in fishing communities and recognizing the continued contribution of women in maintaining the resilience of small-scale fishing communities. Declaring that the dependence of fishing communities on aquatic and coastal living natural resources is shaped by the need to meet life and livelihood in their struggle to eradicate poverty and to secure their well-being as well as to express their cultural and spiritual values. Recognizing the complementarity and interdependency of fisheries-related activities within fishing communities. Recognizing the interconnectedness between the health and well-being of coastal communities and of aquatic ecosystems. (WFFP, 2008, 1)

Some WFFP and WFF members also spoke in the plenary of the FAO conference, including Naseegh Jaffer, from the South African organization Masifundise, and Sherry Pictou, from Bear River First Nation in Canada, who were then co-chairs of WFFP's CC. Jaffer and Pictou, who both went on to play key roles representing the fishers' movements in FAO spaces in the following years, challenged the conference participants to actively implement human rights in fisheries, highlighting that addressing such rights at both the national and international levels was crucial. The FAO conference report, which includes the Bangkok Statement in an appendix, notes:

> At the request of the CSOs, which had organized the pre-conference workshop, a panel [including four WFFP members] presented the background and main contents of the CSO Statement. The Statement originates from a long process of consultations and earlier workshops on the issue of rights and responsibilities — in Cambodia, Chile and Thailand. It reflects the fishers' voices from all around the world. The Statement stresses that human rights of fishing communities are indivisible and that development of responsible and sustainable small-scale and indigenous fisheries is possible only if their political, civil, social, economic and cultural rights are addressed in an integrated manner. It calls for a guarantee of access rights of small-scale and indigenous fishing communities to territories, lands and water on which they have

> traditionally depended for their life and livelihoods. It opposes the privatization of fishery resources through the use of ITQs, and calls for binding involvement of local and indigenous communities in the declaration and establishment of MPAs. (FAO, 2008, 21)

The events that took place in Bangkok gave the fishers' movements a new impetus and were critical for increasing the international visibility of the fishers' movements for two reasons. First, the Bangkok Statement served as the foundation for the development of a set of international guidelines on small-scale fisheries which were envisioned by fishers' organizations themselves. The demands articulated in the Statement presented a unifying vision and a mobilizing force and provided a basis upon which movement members could collaborate at the international level and ensure their voices and perspectives were at the core of the guidelines. Second, the convergence of the fishers' movements and FAO at the Bangkok conference was the beginning of a new chapter in the relationship between the two, in which they had a common goal to engage with, beginning a five-year collaboration toward the development and international endorsement of the guidelines. These two developments in internal capacity-building and alliance-building with FAO were pivotal to the future longevity of the fishers' movements, and they continue to be crucial factors for maintaining movement participation in intergovernmental spaces contributing to the politics of global fisheries.

Developing the Small-Scale Fisheries Guidelines (2009–14)

The year following the Bangkok meetings, WFFP, WFF, ICSF and FAO entered into extensive discussions around developing a set of international guidelines on small-scale fisheries, which would later become the *Voluntary Guidelines for Securing Sustainable Small-Scale Fisheries in the Context of Food Security and Poverty Eradication* (SSF Guidelines) (FAO, 2015; Pictou, 2017). The intention was to present the completed Guidelines for endorsement by FAO's Committee on Fisheries — which as noted earlier is an intergovernmental forum made up of UN Member States where fisheries issues are discussed at the global level and recommendations and policy advice are given to national governments. While some fishers' movement members had participated marginally in COFI sessions since the early 2000s, such direct engagement with this space was a relatively new experience. The development of the Guidelines marked a turning point for the movements in both the COFI space and broader FAO spaces due to their recognition as central actors in the Guidelines process with relevant knowledge and perspectives to contribute. Interviewees pointed out that the COFI space had historically been primarily for discussion between national government delegations, with minimal recognition of social movements.

Sherry Pictou, who together with Naseegh Jaffer played a key role in the negotiation of the Guidelines, noted:

> Over a period of several years, [WFFP, WFF and ICSF], with the assistance of the International Planning Committee for Food Sovereignty (IPC) struggled to develop and have COFI approve a set of guidelines that would protect the rights of SSF. These guidelines were strategically drafted using a human rights-based approach and principles of food security as outlined in the International Guidelines on Responsible Governance of Tenure of Land, Fisheries and Forests, adherence to UNDRIP and to other related international instruments — all in efforts to reprioritize broader community approaches to fishing over neoliberal corporate models. (2017, 3)

Processes for negotiating UN declarations and guidelines have historically been long and arduous — particularly for the social movements that have led civil society efforts toward approval or endorsement. While the UN system, with its efforts to establish global frameworks for the protection of human rights, is the leading institution in universal rights-making, such efforts are also plagued by the voluntary and non-binding nature of many of its instruments (Edelman and James, 2011). This means that while government members of COFI can endorse instruments like the SSF Guidelines, their implementation at national levels is still voluntary and can essentially be carried out as governments see fit. Implementation may also be co-opted by private sector interests to achieve particular goals that benefit companies or generate profits. The process of negotiation is also typically a long-term struggle which often forces participants — particularly social movements — to compromise on many of the details and demands. There is a delicate balance that must be reached between doing justice to civil society perspectives and reflecting a language that is not too radical and is therefore acceptable to the diverse participating governments.

After several years of difficult international negotiations between 2009 and 2014, the SSF Guidelines were endorsed in June 2014 by UN Member States during the 31st COFI Session. The SSF Guidelines are the first international instrument dedicated completely to the small-scale fisheries

Developing the SSF Guidelines (FAO, Rome); back row, left to right: Naseegh Jaffer and Sherry Pictou (WFFP), Margaret Nakato (WFF), Vivienne Solis Rivera and middle row, centre: Chandrika Sharma (ICSF). Source: Johnston, 2012.

sector, and their endorsement marks a pivotal moment and historical achievement for fishers' movements at both the international and national levels. There had long been a critical need for such an instrument, which provides guidance and principles for addressing the challenges faced by small-scale fisheries (WFFP, 2014; FAO, 2015). The endorsement also "created a new 'space' in the international fora, where the protection of rights of small-scale fisheries (SSF) people is promoted, and where indifference, unfairness and injustice within and against SSF are placed under the world's purview" (Nakamura et al., 2021, 1).

The SSF Guidelines bring together the 2008 Bangkok Statement's calls for securing the access rights, post-harvest rights and human rights of small-scale fishers and recommendations emerging from the 29th (2011) and 30th (2012) COFI Sessions. According to FAO, the Guidelines were developed through a participatory and consultative process, facilitated by regional FAO bodies, involving over 4,000 participants from governments, small-scale fishers and fish workers organizations, researchers and development practitioners from over 120 countries. The participants contributed to the process via six regional discussions and more than 20 consultative meetings organized by civil society organizations. The FAO Technical Consultation used the outcome of these meetings to draft the text of the SSF Guidelines between May 2013 and February 2014 (FAO, 2014a; 2015).

Central Themes of the Small-Scale Fisheries Guidelines

1) Responsible fisheries and sustainable development, including:
    a) responsible governance of tenure in small-scale fisheries and sustainable resource management;
    b) social development, employment and decent work;
    c) value chains, post-harvest and trade;
    d) gender equality;
    e) disaster risks and climate change.
2) Ensuring an enabling environment and supporting implementation, including:
    a) policy coherence, institutional coordination and collaboration;
    b) information, research and communication;
    c) capacity development;
    d) implementation support and monitoring. (Source: FAO, 2015)

WFFP, together with ICSF, were key forces driving the development of the SSF Guidelines, playing central roles in the negotiations and advocacy work that took place in the years leading up to the endorsement. One interviewee from WFFP noted that this was extremely hard work and involved putting a lot of pressure on FAO to make sure the demands of the fishers' movements were not watered-down too much. The fishers' movements spent a lot of time strategizing and preparing themselves for the four COFI sessions that took place between 2009 and 2014 and lobbying governments for their support on the sidelines and during breaks from the COFI plenaries (WFFP, 2014). At the 2011 COFI, WFFP was finally able to organize a side event to promote the SSF Guidelines, in collaboration with ICSF, as these events could previously only be organized by FAO, governments and NGOs. In 2012, after being largely inactive since 2004 due to a lack of coordination capacity, WFF re-emerged and began collaborating with WFFP and ICSF on the Guidelines negotiations, which added extra movement power to the process (WFF, 2010).

Several interviewees commented on how the process of collaboration between WFFP, WFF and ICSF around the SSF Guidelines was key to building strength and solidarity, both within and between the organizations. One WFFP member noted:

Small-scale fisheries side event at COFI (Rome), including (left to right) Brian O'Riordan (ICSF), Herman Kumara (WFFP), Rolf Willmann (FAO), Chandrika Sharma (ICSF), Naseegh Jaffer (WFFP) and Margaret Nakato (WFF) Source: Johnston, 2012.

> We spent a lot of time on that. I think what we did together with the other groups was quite good. We know it's a guideline, it's not a law, but I'm proud of what we did, to actually have brought it from nothing to what it eventually became… I think bringing in the small-scale where it was previously only about big business, bringing in the small-scale was a victory for us. And I think WFF, WFFP and ICSF should be proud of that. We should be proud of what we did there.

Some interviewees commented on the indispensable role in the Guidelines process of the executive secretary of ICSF at the time, Chandrika Sharma, who was a passionate and dedicated organizer working with fishing communities in India and globally. She was a driving force, facilitator and mobilizer who had been advocating for the Guidelines since the beginning. Tragically, Sharma was aboard Malaysian Airlines flight MH370, which disappeared in March 2014 — just three months before the Guidelines she had fought so hard for were endorsed. Sharma's disappearance had an immeasurable impact on the transnational fishers' movements and the fishing communities she worked with, and this impact continues to be felt within the network. She had been a central link between ICSF, WFFP and WFF and had a unique combination of passion, devotion and the ability to bring people together that is crucial in building and maintaining organizational relationships. In recognition of Sharma's central and invaluable role, both the fishers' movements and the Norwegian government proposed that the Guidelines be adopted in Chandrika's name. The dedication of the SSF Guidelines reads: "In honour of Chandrika Sharma, who worked tirelessly for the betterment of the lives of fish workers all over the world and who contributed invaluably to the formulation of the Guidelines" (FAO, 2015, iii).

Post-Guidelines Endorsement and Ongoing Challenges (2014–20)

Although the endorsement of the SSF Guidelines was considered a crucial victory for the fishers' movements following five years of intensive work and difficult negotiations, the next big challenge would be international implementation. Despite their approval of the SSF Guidelines in COFI, many governments do not prioritize the implementation of voluntary instruments or end up implementing them in ways that are not holistic or are moulded to their own interests. Co-optation also becomes a risk once guidelines reach a certain amount of international prominence and various actors see involvement in their implementation as a potential vehicle for promoting their own interests or receiving government funding or private sector investment. The continuation of the collaborative effort that began during the Guidelines development, in particular the participation of small-scale fishers' organizations, is crucial for the Guidelines to be successfully implemented and retain their relevance (Singleton et al., 2017). Yet, maintaining the same level of collaboration is no easy feat, particularly within transnational fishers' movements, as the development of the Guidelines involved a clear common task and goal of endorsement, while implementation must take different forms depending on the regional and national context. It is more difficult to build a common international vision around which to mobilize transnationally, making the implementation process one that movements have to take up at the national level. This diverts attention and already limited organizational funds away from international advocacy and capacity-building, toward national fisheries policy and local empowerment to understand and engage with the Guidelines (Claeys and Edelman, 2020). In the post-2014 period, this would prove to be a key challenge for maintaining energy in the transnational fishers' movements.

Propelled by the momentum that was built around developing and endorsing the SSF Guidelines, energy and mobilization remained relatively high in the fishers' movements in the following few years. Between 2014 and 2016 in particular, many events and meetings were organized, and

WFFP and WFF continued working toward strengthening a collaborative relationship. However, the endorsement of the SSF Guidelines was only the first step toward having a functioning international instrument that would prioritize and uphold the rights of small-scale fishing communities. In the first three years after their endorsement, while there were some efforts to exchange knowledge and success stories among communities, most of the implementation activities revolved around incorporating the Guidelines into regional and national legislation. While this is certainly important for FAO's intergovernmental mandate and the long-term enforceability of the Guidelines, it fails to address the issue that small-scale fishing communities have historically been overlooked by national governments and laws (Singleton et al., 2017). Singleton et al. argue:

> If the SSF-Guidelines are to have relevance to and material impact on the lives of small-scale fishers, it is vital that more attention is urgently paid to implementation from the ground up, and to linking national, international and regional efforts with such efforts in small-scale fishing communities. The question then arises: How can this be achieved with any expediency, when national Governments (especially in developing countries, where most small-scale fisheries are located) are unlikely to be able to divert time and resources, and may not have the necessary relationships of trust, to start working with small-scale fishing communities overnight? (2017, 22)

Ebbs and Flows in Transnational Mobilization

After the excitement of the Guidelines endorsement started to wear off and attention shifted toward national-level implementation, proactiveness and mobilization in the transnational fishers' movements began to wane. Some interviewees noted that, after the Guidelines were endorsed, there was a kind of "now what?" moment, when they no longer felt they had a common goal to work toward at the international level. Many movement members said it was a good time to scale back and focus on SSF Guidelines implementation in their own countries, national-level work and local fisheries issues. This shift in the intensity of international mobilization is reflective of what social movement scholars describe as protest cycles, or the regular ebbs and flows of social movements over time (Tarrow, 2011; McAdam, 1995). Tarrow explains that this can make it more difficult to maintain steady or constant mobilization within a movement:

> The solutions to the problem of mobilizing people into campaigns and coalitions of collective action depend on shared understandings, social networks, and connective structures and the use of culturally resonant forms of action. But above all… they are triggered by the ebb and flow of political struggle. (2011, 16)

Ebbs and flows may be influenced by external global politics, internal member dynamics, organizational capacities, available time and funding cycles, among other things (Tarrow, 2011). In the context of fishers' movements, which are relatively small in comparison to agrarian movements like LVC, the core group of active members involved in the development of the SSF Guidelines had expended a significant amount of their time, energy and organizational resources on the process, and some understandably needed to regroup and refocus their attention to issues closer to home. A few members, however, used the internal strength and capacity of their organizations to maintain some momentum and keep tabs on fisheries governance processes and debates taking place at the international level. One initiative several WFF and WFFP members started working on with FAO in 2016 was the establishment of the Global Strategic Framework (SSF-GSF), a mechanism to support the implementation of the SSF Guidelines at all levels, which movement members would guide as part of the Advisory Group (FAO, 2018c).[3] From WFF, two member organizations that participated in this initiative and remained active in international spaces were the Tanzanian Environment Management and Economic Development Organisation (EMEDO) and the Ugandan Katosi Women Development Trust (KWDT). These members were both part of WFF's Executive Committee at the time (2012–17) and were represented by Editrudith Lukanga (EMEDO) as the co-president, and Margaret Nakato (KWDT) as the executive director. Both Lukanga and Nakato had begun collaborating with WFFP and ICSF to develop the Guidelines in 2012 when WFF joined the process.

From WFFP, a member that continued to play a fundamental role in international spaces and developing the SSF-GSF was Masifundise, a South African organization of which Naseegh Jaffer is the director. As discussed earlier, Jaffer had been centrally involved in the development of the SSF Guidelines from their initial inception at the 2008 Bangkok meeting and had become skilled in understanding and engaging with international processes, particularly within FAO. Masifundise also served as WFFP's general secretary from 2014 to 2017 and devoted a lot of time and energy to ensuring that there were representatives present in important international fisheries spaces, creating strong communication channels between the members and developing a strategy for capacity-building within other member organizations. They also strengthened existing relationships with allied organizations, established new alliances and organized two WFFP General Assemblies, in 2014 and 2017, both of which included participation from WFF and a large number of allied groups. The 6th WFFP General Assembly, hosted by Masifundise in Cape Town, South Africa, in September 2014, brought together 100 delegates from over 30 countries, as well as many representatives from local South African fishers' organizations. In the General Assembly report, Jaffer highlighted the tremendous benefits that belonging to WFFP holds for local organizations: "It provides solidarity, we can take similar positions on issues, we can learn from each other's struggles, build a strong social movement and together learn to bring about change that will benefit fishing communities locally and internationally" (WFFP, 2014, 4).

Despite some ebbs in transnational mobilization that occurred within the fishers' movements, both in the pre- and post-Guidelines endorsement periods, there were still numerous important meetings organized. WFFP consistently held annual CC meetings and triennial General Assemblies, including in Kisumu, Kenya (2004), Negombo, Sri Lanka (2007), Karachi, Pakistan (2011), and Cape Town, South Africa (2014), with the most recent one in New Delhi, India (2017), celebrating the 20th anniversary of the 1st General Assembly in the same city. Due to the COVID-19 pandemic, the 2020 General Assembly, which was to take place in Brazil, had to be postponed (WFFP, 2020d). In contrast, WFF had been largely inactive until 2012, when it joined the SSF Guidelines process, and noted in its 2010 annual report that it had been focusing on strengthening its secretariat, since the organization had "been loosely networked for the past 6 years since its last General Assembly in 2004," with only a few of its members actively representing fisher folk in small-scale fisheries arenas (WFF, 2010, 3). However, around 2012, WFF became more active, holding General Assemblies in Kampala, Uganda (2012) and Salinas, Ecuador (2017) and planned regular CC and Executive Committee meetings (WFF, 2020d).

The preceding sections describe some of the key similarities and differences between WFFP and WFF as they have evolved into the movements they are today and pinpoint important convergences with international allies. Fishers' movements have also been visible actors in the politics of global fisheries, a role which is partially illuminated by their historical evolution and movement-building processes. Three pivotal developments help us understand fishers' movements' political agendas and alliance-building strategies.

Pivotal Developments for Political Agendas and Alliance-Building

The emergence and evolution of WFF and WFFP, including ebbs and flows in their level of mobilization, internal capacity and international visibility, have been influenced by structural and institutional transformations in global fisheries. Fishers' movements have responded to such transformations and related marginalization of small-scale fishers by developing new ways to amplify their voices, build their international networks, strengthen their alliances and engage in strategic spaces and platforms. In the context of the rapidly globalizing world of the 1990s and early 2000s and the increasing prominence of UN bodies such as FAO and the Intergovernmental Panel on Climate Change (IPCC), these organizations became increasingly involved in integrating a wide range of global actors, such as fishers' movements, in political processes (Tarrow, 2005; Smith and Guarnizo, 2006). In this context, the idea of transnational has been useful for those concerned with extending human rights and political and social equality beyond nation-state borders (Fox, 2005). Fishers' movements recognized transnational citizenship as a strategic avenue for scaling up their struggles for fisheries justice and linking up with like-minded resource justice allies and sympathetic international organizations. As Fox argues, "the rise of transnational civil society and an associated public sphere is extending claims to membership in cross-border civic and political communities grounded in rights-based worldviews, such as feminism, environmentalism, indigenous rights, and human rights" (2005, 173). Important insights can therefore be gained from the transnational experiences of fishers' movements, particularly in relation to three pivotal developments: 1) their internalization of overlapping fisheries, food and climate crises; 2) transnational agrarian movements increasing engagement with the fisheries aspects of converging food and climate crises; and 3) intergovernmental UN bodies broadening their attention to fisheries issues (Mills, 2022).

Fishers' Movements Internalizing Overlapping Global Crises

Fishers' movements have increasingly internalized the overlap of the fisheries, food and climate crises and are aligning their activities and demands accordingly by putting food and climate issues forward as central pillars of their agendas (Mills, 2022). Food sovereignty, for instance, which strives for food and climate justice, has become an important mobilization tool, analytical guide and alternative that fishers' movements have been engaging with since the 2008 Bangkok Statement. Food sovereignty involves people's right to both healthy and culturally appropriate food which is produced using ecological and sustainable methods, as well as to define their own food production systems. In the context of food systems and policies, food sovereignty also prioritizes the needs and aspirations of the food producers, distributors and consumers over the demands of markets and corporations (Nyéléni, 2007). As a counter-narrative, food sovereignty challenges the corporate-controlled food system and is a response to late 1970s neoliberal globalization, which contributed to fragmenting rural labour, weakening workers' unions, privatizing industries and intensifying international competition (Edelman and Borras, 2016; Smith, 2013; Scholte, 2011). The concept of food sovereignty was first introduced by LVC in 1996 at the World Food Summit in Rome and within a few years gained traction with a wide range of rural food producers (Claeys and Duncan, 2019). In the context of fisheries, Levkoe et al. argue:

> Food sovereignty helps to explore the complexities embodied in a fish as food approach, including the interconnections between social, ecological and economic wellbeing as well as governance structures. Using this perspective draws attention to the way that fisheries are power laden and subject to the neoliberal logics of the corporate, industrial food system. Food sovereignty demands that fisheries be conceived as part of complex social and ecological systems and that there must be a more central role for community-based, small scale fishers in decision-making surrounding management. (2017, 66)

Transnational fishers' movements, which are concerned about the broad impacts of neoliberalism and climate change on fishing communities, have mobilized around food sovereignty, arguing that it is an effective long-term solution and away forward (WFFP, 2020a; Barbesgaard, 2018). For the past decade, fishers' movements have engaged with food sovereignty through their participation in the IPC by establishing a food sovereignty working group in 2015 and publishing a report entitled *Agroecology and Food Sovereignty in Small-Scale Fisheries* in 2017. This report defines food sovereignty as "a political agenda of small-scale food producers in defence of our rivers, lakes, oceans and land. It is a response to the encroachment of our food system by multinational corporations who, in the context of fisheries, seek to privatize and consolidate fishing rights in the hands of a few" (KNTI and WFFP, 2017, 4). The report further notes:

> For more than a decade, WFFP has engaged in dialogues with other social movements and ally NGOs through the International Planning Committee on Food Sovereignty and other spaces. Those conversations were vital to the learning and reflection of fishing communities around the themes of Food Sovereignty and Agroecology. Also, WFFP was able to influence the debate and include the voices and experiences of fisher people in exchanges and related policies. As a global social movement, WFFP is committed to sharing information and nourishing the debate around these two important topics in fishing communities. (17)

During WFFP's 7th General Assembly, in India in November 2017, where WFF members also participated, a workshop discussed the report and unpacked how small-scale fishers relate to food sovereignty. Participants reflected on their own local contexts and experiences with food sovereignty, with one participant commenting:

> We have always understood food production is our right, and it is about not destroying our fish stocks and our natural environment. It is also about how to control and manage that production and make sure destructive practices stay out. It is about how we take joint and collaborative decisions about production. It is about our culture and belief systems. It is about how particular species or marine life interact with our daily lives. This is what we have always known, but we just never called it food sovereignty before — we always had the same principles but just used different language.

Yet, the food sovereignty discussion within fisheries is not without its challenges, particularly when scaling it down from the level of international debate to tangible activities at the national level. WFFP noted:

> In the context of national organizations, members of WFFP, more time is needed to deepen and build the understanding of Agroecology and Food Sovereignty. We would like to encourage the organization of learning exchanges between and led by fishing communities, documentation of best practices and debates among WFFP members, and communication strategies to disseminate information about Food Sovereignty and Agroecology to fishing families. A good communication strategy is also important to support the organizing of local communities so they can advocate for

> their rights in the face of threats created by multinational corporations. (KNTI and WFFP, 2017, 17)

The issue of international trade also complicates food sovereignty discussions in fisheries, considering many fishers around the world depend on selling their catches to the international market — an element which some movement members do not feel is adequately addressed in food sovereignty debates. Several participants at the 2017 food sovereignty workshop argued that their livelihoods depend on catching species which are not eaten locally, such as octopus, and they felt that food sovereignty is too focused on the localization of food. This localization issue reflects a contradiction in agrarian food systems as well. As Robbins (2015) argues, local food systems alone are not enough to challenge the global industrial food system, and even a local food system that fits an ideal food sovereignty type does not constitute food sovereignty in and of itself. Therefore, if food sovereignty is to have long-term, wide-reaching mobilization power among fishers' movements, this discussion needs to continue, both within fishers' movements and more broadly, with more attention to which aspects are useful in the fisheries context and which are not.

Fishers' movements' internalization of overlapping fisheries, food and climate crises, and mobilization around food sovereignty demonstrates their commitment to participating in, and shaping, the future of the fisheries sector and its socio-political context in a way that addresses their specific concerns. Through their trajectories of resistance, fishers' movements are becoming increasingly intertwined with other resource justice movements, particularly agrarian movements, and implicated in debates around food and climate politics. This has facilitated a convergence of strategies for achieving both structural and tactical change by building new societal models and alternative food systems (Claeys and Duncan, 2019). These alliances, particularly at the transnational level, are crucial for movements in navigating multiple levels of social organization (global, national, local), developing stronger and more efficient negotiation tools and learning from each other's experiences (Rivera-Ferre et al., 2014).

Convergence of Fishers' and Agrarian Movements and Platforms

The second pivotal development is that transnational agrarian movements, such as LVC, and the international platforms they participate in, namely the IPC and the Civil Society and Indigenous Peoples Mechanism (CSM), are increasingly engaging with fisheries issues (discussed in detail in the next chapter) (Mills, 2022). This is reflected in the issues and demands they raise and the convergence of fishers' and agrarian movements in various events and spaces. This convergence focuses on building food systems that are based on food sovereignty and agroecology models and centred on small-scale food producers' access to and control over land and natural resources (Tramel, 2018; GRtFN, 2015). The convergence of fishers and agrarian movements is therefore strongly linked to the global food sovereignty movement, which, as Claeys and Duncan argue, has "over the last three decades, created and in different ways enforced, systems of categorization to build unity and convergence between different participant movements, while negotiating and maintaining differences" (2019, 1). Convergence between movements illuminates a common thread linking agrarian and fisheries justice issues and marks an important opportunity for collaboration between these movements. Together they call into question current modes of production, distribution and consumption in the global food system as central threats to the health of the global environment and climate (Tramel, 2018).

Efforts to enhance the alliance between agrarian and fishers' movements was evident at the launch of the Global Convergence of Land and Water Struggles during the March 2015 World Social Forum in Tunisia. The joint declaration emerging from this convergence demonstrates that collaborations between social movements and organizations engaged in defending land and water rights recognize the vital link between land and water struggles, particularly the increasing and overlapping threat of land and water grabbing globally (see LVC, 2015a). The convergence of agrarian and fishers' movements is also evident within the IPC, which is an international CSO network established in 1996 that LVC, WFFP and WFF are all members of. The IPC brings together organizations representing farmers, fishers, agricultural workers, Indigenous Peoples and NGOs and provides a common space for mobilization that links local struggles and global debate. Since 2002, the IPC has also been the official platform coordinating civil society participation in some FAO processes, such as COFI and the Committee on World Food Security (CFS) (IPC, 2017, see also Chapter 4).

In March 2018, Masifundise, as a member of WFFP and its 2014–17 secretariat, hosted the biennial IPC General Meeting in South Africa. Several social movement representatives present noted that they were impressed with the organization of the meeting and with the strong voices of WFFP members, commenting that the exchanges that took place helped to strengthen the alliance between WFFP and agrarian movements. Some participants further pointed out that the role of fishers' movements in the

IPC space has contributed to increasing the visibility of fisheries issues in the IPC and FAO processes and spaces. Despite these important gains in alliance-building between fishers' and agrarian movements in recent years, there is still work to be done in strengthening modes of communication and collaboration between them and, as one WFFP member told me, for fishers' movements to "really learn from the experiences of farmers' movements in scaling up our struggles more visibly at the global level." Such alliances can make important contributions in fisheries and in the global food system more broadly, in which small-scale producers are increasingly able to demand recognition of their rights, secure access to resources and participation in decision-making processes at the local, national and transnational levels.

Transnational movements offer spaces to address threats stemming from converging fisheries, food and climate crises, among diverse groups of people from different cultures and epistemologies, from every corner of the globe. They offer the possibility of uniting representatives from diverse social groups to "debate, analyze, strategize, build consensus around collective readings of reality, and agree on collective actions and campaigns with national, regional, continental, or global scope" (Rosset and Martinez-Torres, 2014, 138). Transnational movements and their alliances have also contributed to

> reframing the terms and parameters of a wide range of debates and practices in the field of international development, including environmental sustainability and climate change, land rights and redistributive agrarian reform, food sovereignty, neoliberal economics and global trade rules, corporate control of crop genetic material and other agricultural technology, the human rights of peasants and gender equity. For policymakers, scholars, activists and development practitioners concerned with these issues, an understanding of [transnational movements] and their impact is essential for grasping interconnections between these thematic areas and between these and the "big picture" as well. (Edelman and Borras, 2016, 1)

In the context of the global food sovereignty movement, and more specifically within the IPC, two tools have been particularly useful for movement actors:

> They have used constituency categories (for example, pastoralists, fishers, Indigenous Peoples, agricultural workers, small-holder farmers, women and youth) to identify, protect, foster and guar-

> antee autonomy of movements and organizations representing different groups of people with distinct identities and lived realities. They have also used quotas (for example, gender, age, constituency and/or geography) to protect diversity, prevent the consolidation of power, and ensure the prioritized participation of affected or marginalized groups within the Movement, notably over NGOs. The use of constituencies and quotas has supported two distinct but related objectives of the movement: alliances building and effective direct representation in global policy-making spaces. (Claeys and Duncan, 2019, 1)

These tools have been particularly useful in intergovernmental spaces at the UN level, namely within FAO, which in the last decade has increasingly created space for civil society participation. Intergovernmental processes are complex, involving a diverse range of actors and knowledge, and movement participation in these spaces certainly involves tensions. Yet, despite the divergences and conflicts that can emerge between movements, global convergence around processes and goals has become an important unifying and mobilization strategy that is increasingly linking fishers' and agrarian movements.

Intergovernmental Bodies Addressing Fisheries Issues

The third pivotal development is that key intergovernmental bodies within the UN, such as FAO and IPCC, have increased attention to fisheries in their analyses and activities (Mills, 2022). UN bodies have become important spaces for transnational movement engagement since they began opening up to civil society participation in the midst of 1990s globalization and the shift towards global governance. The UN system, which had been somewhat of a government fortress since its founding in 1945, began to recognize that there was a need to move away from secretive, closed-door intergovernmental processes and involve a more diverse range of actors. In 1992, the Commission on Global Governance was established, and the 1990s became the decade of UN global summits, which provided an opportunity to rethink strict intergovernmental approaches and extend an unprecedented invitation to CSOs (Civil Society Organizations). While the closed-door negotiation of the Millennium Development Goals (MDGs) was a disappointment to CSOs, the global food and agriculture agenda centred in FAO offered a promising channel of engagement for food producers' organizations (McKeon, 2017a; Scholte, 2011).

Another key factor in movements' participation in UN spaces was their increasing recognition of the transnational value of the human rights framework, which is at the core of much of the UN's discourse. Smith (1998) notes that between the 1970s and 90s, more than a quarter of transnational movements focused their work on human rights issues (47). By the 2000s, CSOs working on food issues and agrarian and fishers' movements increasingly engaged with this framework, particularly when dealing with the impacts of neoliberal processes on small-scale food producers and framing their demands for secure livelihoods and food security. This approach allowed them to gain space and legitimacy in the international system and extend their participation beyond the scope of traditional state-based representation (Marchetti, 2017).

Several examples illustrate increasing engagement between intergovernmental bodies and fisheries issues. The increased participation of fishers' movements in certain intergovernmental spaces has arguably contributed to this increased engagement by raising the profile of small-scale fisheries and drawing attention to the demands of the movements. For example, members of both WFFP and WFF have been participating in CFS via the CSM since its establishment in 2010. WFFP and WFF each have one member participating in the Coordination Committee of the CSM, which is the largest international space of CSOs working to eradicate food insecurity and malnutrition (FAO, 2021d). There has also been greater attention to the protection of fisheries resources and areas in UN agendas. The most prominent example of this is the inclusion of Goal 14: Life Below Water in the UN's Sustainable Development Goals, which were adopted by the General Assembly in 2015 and are a central pillar guiding IPCC assessments (see IPCC, 2018). More importantly, Goal 14 includes Target 14.B to "provide access for small-scale artisanal fishers to marine resources and markets," and countries' progress will be indicated by the application of legal, regulatory, policy and institutional frameworks that recognize and protect small-scale fishers' access rights (UN, 2015a). The 2014 endorsement of the SSF Guidelines was a major achievement for fishers' movements because it demonstrated national governments' recognition of the importance of the small-scale sector. The subsequent 2018 adoption of the UN *Declaration on the Rights of Peasants and Other People Working in Rural Areas* (UNDROP), a high-level international governance instrument that was written by and for small-scale producers, was also a historical event and a landmark achievement for both agrarian and fishers' movements (FAO, 2018a; Claeys and Edelman, 2020).

There were three important antecedents for the human rights framing in the SSF Guidelines: 1) the institutionalization of human rights approaches to development in the UN system, which gives particular attention to the Right to Food; 2) the recognition that small-scale fishers, including Indigenous groups, are typically socially, economically and politically marginalized and face numerous obstacles to participating in decision-making processes; and 3) the rise of social movements that recognize and secure the traditional and communal tenure systems of small-scale producers and Indigenous Peoples, in opposition to initiatives aiming to expand state ownership and private property rights over land, water and other resources (Ratner et al., 2014). Fishers' movements have recognized that a human rights–based approach provides a means of tackling the social, economic and political marginalization of small-scale fishers by "addressing the root causes of these inequities, which lie in unequal power relations and the failure of states and other powerful non-state actors to respect and uphold the rights of all citizens" (Ratner et al., 2014, 121). WFFP et al. (2016) further define the three main criteria of a human rights–based approach to fisheries: First, it must be multi-dimensional and holistic, meaning all human rights are interrelated, interdependent and indivisible and must be respected and upheld equally. Second, it must have a pro-poor stance on decision-making and impact, meaning the most marginalized communities and individuals within communities must receive extra attention to ensure their rights are respected. Third, it must involve an accountability structure in which the state is the key duty bearer, meaning nation states play a central role in respecting and protecting human rights, particularly due to their membership in the UN and related international treaties and obligations.

While participation in intergovernmental spaces has not always been an easy or positive experience for fishers' movements, such spaces have been critical to both developing their political agendas and strengthening their alliances with UN bodies — especially FAO. As Smith (1998) argues, transnational movements' structures and activities help activists to familiarize themselves with the ways that intergovernmental institutions function and develop skills to be able to work effectively within them. Movement participation in their own regional and international meetings allows members to gain experience engaging with global political processes and strengthen their ability to make strategic connections between national and international issues and agendas. Fishers' movements' engagement in intergovernmental spaces certainly has become stronger over time, as they have honed their political strategies and knowledge of global processes. Chapter 4 picks up on this discussion, exploring the ways in which movements are engaging with intergovernmental bodies and participating in political spaces and the challenges they are encountering.

Concluding Remarks

The road to establishing a transnational movement and maintaining its unity and momentum over time is one replete with bumps and crossroads. Considering the diversity of members comprising the fishers' movements, the 2000 split in Loctudy, occurring largely due to political and personal clashes and disagreement about the movement's structure and membership base, was considered inevitable by some members. Tensions around movement boundaries and who or what has the privilege of being included in a movement presents a dilemma that has been analyzed in social movement literature for decades. Members within a movement often have conflicting ideas about political strategy, how inclusive to be and what criteria should determine membership. The key questions that emerged from this critical moment in fishers' movement history include whether there may have been a different outcome had there been different actors in leadership roles. Similarly, would a split still have occurred if there were more members with neutral positions in the conflict, meaning without strong loyalties to particular individuals, or more members playing peacekeeping roles? Did the split have any long-term impacts on the transnational strength of the two emerging movements? If WFF and WFFP members had remained united, could the movement have evolved into one with a broader membership base and a wider international reach — similar to its agrarian ally, LVC? These are of course retrospective questions which can only be answered speculatively but are interesting to reflect upon nonetheless.

The evolution of WFFP and WFF in the years that followed the 2000 split was punctuated by a great deal of mobilization and energy leading up to and during the development of the SSF Guidelines. There were also key individuals propelling this process from both the fishers' movements and support organizations, without which the Guidelines may never have been endorsed by COFI members or may have ended up taking a form that was much less reflective of the movement perspective. Centring the Guidelines on a human rights–based approach was an important strategic direction which further strengthened fishers' movements' relationship with UN bodies like FAO and enhanced their capacities to engage with and negotiate in intergovernmental spaces. The post-Guidelines endorsement period since 2014 has raised a lot of questions for fishers' movements about how to maintain the momentum they built around the Guidelines development, while ensuring the Guidelines are implemented at the national level in a way that truly reflects the holistic human rights principles they are built upon. While the process of developing the Guidelines involved a clear common goal which fostered unity within and between WFFP, WFF, ICSF, FAO and others, the implementation process takes many different forms in diverse national contexts. This makes it difficult to maintain the same level of transnational mobilization within the movements, first because it is harder to pinpoint a clear common pathway toward implementation that such a diverse membership can rally around and second because many members are busy working with local fishers' organizations and governments in the national implementation process. These challenges are part of the natural ebbs and flows that emerge at different political moments and determine how active movements remain over time (Tarrow, 2011).

For fishers' movements, the need to collect and preserve historical and archival data is critical. This is important both as a publicly available resource which researchers and other interested actors can access and as a critical tool for movement-building among the members themselves. Many of the people who were involved in the early days of establishing and building the fishers' movements have either retired from movement life or have passed away. This makes the transfer of knowledge between old and new members to prevent the loss of important organizational and institutional knowledge difficult, yet urgent. The evolution of the fishers' movements, as with all social movements, has been full of lessons learned, political agendas and strategies developed, tensions and obstacles overcome and victories won. These elements have been woven together to create the historical, social and political fabric of the movements, a fabric unique to WFF and WFFP. In order for current or new members to truly understand what the movement is built upon and what is stands for, it is critical that these historical intricacies be shared more widely and openly between members. While it is certainly important for movements not to dwell too much on the past and to continue to move forward, the movement-building process itself can also provide valuable fuel to keep political momentum going well into the future.

Table 3.3: Timeline of Key Events for Fishers' Movements (1984–2021)

Event	Place	Date
International Conference of Fishworkers and their Supporters	FAO, Rome, Italy	July 1984
Trivandrum Workshop — Towards an International Collective in Support of Fishworkers (ICSF)	Trivandrum, India	November 1986
International Symposium on Marine Environment and the Future of Fishworkers	Lisbon, Portugal	June 1989
Global Fisheries Trends and the Future of Fishworkers (international conference)	Bangkok, Thailand	January 1990
Cebu Conference	Cebu, Philippines	June 1994
World Trade Organization establishment	Geneva, Switzerland	January 1995
1st WFF General Assembly (establishment); 1st Coordination Committee Meeting	New Delhi, India	November 1997
2nd WFF Coordination Committee Meeting (Namur Meeting)	Namur, Belgium	October 1998
3rd WFF Coordination Committee Meeting (San Francisco Meeting)	San Francisco, USA	October 1999
Battle of Seattle protests	Seattle, USA	November – December 1999
4th WFF Coordination Committee Meeting	Loctudy, France	April 2000
2nd WFF General Assembly, WFFP-WFF Split (2nd WFFP General Assembly)	Loctudy, France	October 2000
1st WFFP Coordination Committee meeting	Mumbai (Bombay), India	March 2001
World Summit on Sustainable Development; Global Peoples Forum (parallel)	Johannesburg, South Africa	August – September 2002
2nd WFFP Coordination Committee Meeting	Fort de France, Martinique	April 2002
International Fisherfolk Workshop	Bali, Indonesia	June 2002
3rd WFFP Coordination Committee Meeting	Nainamadama, Sri Lanka	June, 2003

Event	Place	Date
World Trade Organization Conference	Cancun, Mexico	September 2003
3rd WFF General Assembly	Lisbon, Portugal	2004
3rd WFFP General Assembly	Kisumu, Kenya	November 2004
4th WFFP Coordination Committee Meeting	Hong Kong	December 2005
4th WFFP General Assembly	Negombo, Sri Lanka	December 2007
Global Conference on Small-Scale Fisheries	Bangkok, Thailand	October 2008
29th COFI Session	Rome, Italy	March 2009
30th COFI Session	Rome, Italy	February 2011
5th WFFP General Assembly	Karachi, Pakistan	April 2011
31st COFI Session	Rome, Italy	June 2012
4th WFF General Assembly	Kampala, Uganda	November 2012
32nd COFI Session (Small-Scale Fisheries Guidelines endorsement)	Rome, Italy	July 2014
6th WFFP General Assembly	Cape Town, South Africa	September 2014
41st CFS Session	Rome, Italy	October 2014
42nd CFS Session	Rome, Italy	October 2015
COP 21; Zone of Action for the Climate (parallel)	Paris, France	December 2015
33rd COFI Session	Rome, Italy	July 2016
43rd CFS Session	Rome, Italy	October 2016
COP 22	Marrakech, Morocco	November 2016
5th WFF General Assembly	Salinas, Ecuador	January 2017
44th CFS Session	Rome, Italy	October 2017
COP 23	Bonn, Germany	November 2017
7th WFFP General Assembly (20th anniversary)	New Delhi, India	November 2017
33rd COFI Session and political trainings	Rome, Italy	July 2018
45th CFS Session	Rome, Italy	October 2018
COP 24	Katowice, Poland	December 2018
46th CFS Session	Rome, Italy	October 2019
COP 25	Madrid, Spain	December 2019

Event	Place	Date
34th COFI Session	Online (Rome)	February 2021
47th CFS Session	Online (Rome)	February 2021

Note: This timeline of key events that fishers' movements participated in between 1984 and 2021 helps to illustrate the link between the historical evolution of the movements with the discussion on international political spaces and processes in the following chapter.

NOTES

1. The term "fishworker" was commonly used among these organizations in the 1980s in order to include different types of workers in the small-scale fisheries sector, namely fishers, fishing crew, processors and sellers. The emergence of WFF and WFFP also added "fish harvesters" and "fisher peoples" to the terms used within the network. However, in spoken language today, the terms "fishers" and "fisherfolk" are most commonly used as a way to encapsulate the range of actors represented by the movements. I use the term "fishers" throughout this book in the interest of consistency, except when referring to quotes or specific reports.
2. The Voluntary Guidelines for Securing Sustainable Small-Scale Fisheries in the Context of Food Security and Poverty Eradication (SSF Guidelines) process is discussed later in this chapter.
3. The SSF-GSF is discussed in Chapter 4.

International Political Spaces

Movements as Actors in Fisheries, Food and Climate Governance

A key element of understanding why and how transnational fishers' movements contest and seek to influence the politics of global fisheries is recognizing the spaces they engage with. Fishers' movements have been prioritizing the following three international political spaces, all of which include participation by CSOs, government delegations, NGOs, researchers and private sector representatives:

1) *Fisheries governance space*: the Committee on Fisheries (COFI) of the United Nations' FAO, an international intergovernmental forum that examines fisheries and aquaculture issues, negotiates global agreements and instruments, and makes recommendations to governments, regional fisheries bodies, NGOs, fish workers and the international community;
2) *Food governance space:* the Committee on World Food Security (CFS) of the United Nations, which reviews and follows up on food security policies, such as those addressing production and access; and
3) *Climate governance space*: the Conference of the Parties (COP) to the United Nations Framework Convention on Climate Change (UNFCCC), which is the principal global decision-making body on national emission limits and climate change mitigation and adaptation goals.

The focus throughout this book on global politics and governance arenas, rather than national politics and the role of the nation state, stems from the globalized context from which transnational movements have emerged. This context challenges political theory "to go beyond a narrow state-centred approach by considering political communities and systems of rights that emerge at levels of governance above or below those of independent states or that cut across international borders" (Bauböck, 2003, 704). While some approaches to understanding movements focus on local situations and actions, the shift of power from nation states to more globalized actors and international institutions, particularly since the 1990s, has required struggles for participation to also engage at the global level (Gaventa, 2006; Edelman, 1999). The shift of both governance and movement engagement toward global arenas also sparked widespread academic interest in trying to understand the consequences of this shift alongside the rapid expansion of neoliberal globalization. Three factors contributed to this growing interest: the increased flow of capital, goods, services and people that globalization allowed; expectations that international organizations would become more prominent in the post-Cold War era; and recognition that a coordinated approach would be needed to address global environmental and climate issues (Marchetti, 2017). In the past few decades, there has been an unprecedented expansion of global governance arenas, such as the UN and agencies like the World Bank and WTO, which have also become increasingly implicated in social struggles in every corner of the globe. Scholte argues:

> These proliferating and growing global-scale regimes have not replaced nation-state and local authorities, which on the whole remain as vibrant as ever. However, global governance has become highly significant in contemporary history, even if the various institutional frameworks show no signs of coalescing to form a world government, in the sense of a sovereign state scaled up to planetary proportions. (2011, 1)

A central element in global governance processes is the political spaces in which diverse actors engage. In the context of citizen action and participation, political "spaces are seen as opportunities, moments and channels where citizens can act to potentially affect policies, discourses, decisions and relationships that affect their lives and interests" (Gaventa, 2006, 26). These can take the form of *closed spaces*, involving decisions being made by powerful actors behind closed doors without any intention of "broadening the boundaries for inclusion"; *invited spaces*, involving people being invited to participate by more powerful actors, such as governments, intergovernmental agencies and NGOs; and *claimed/created spaces*, involving less powerful actors claiming spaces from or against powerful actors or creating autonomous spaces of their own (Gaventa, 2006). In the context of COFI, CFS and COP, fishers' movements have not only strategically targeted these spaces, they have succeeded in gaining access, which is not always easy or possible. While there are many other international spaces that play an important role in fisheries politics — which are not the focus of this book, such as Our Oceans summits, World Ocean summits, Sustainable Development Goals summits, Blue Economy conferences — fishers' movements have typically not participated directly in these. This is either because the movements have not had the capacity to engage or have chosen not to engage, or the spaces are closed and movements have been excluded from them.

COFI, CFS and COP also provide convergence spaces for transnational movements to interact with like-minded groups, discuss and develop collective strategies to address common issues and obstacles and build alliances. Two key convergence spaces for fishers' movements are the International Planning Committee for Food Sovereignty (IPC), through which they engage in COFI; and the Civil Society and Indigenous Peoples Mechanism (CSM), through which they engage in CFS. Exploring such spaces allows us to "interpret the operational and spatial dynamics, strategies, practices and governance arrangements of place-based movements and groups involved in extending their reach" (Claeys and Duncan, 2019, 3). Such spaces typically involve movements that are placed-based, but not necessarily place-bound; allow actors to develop collective visions and identify unifying values; and require relational solidarity politics that link movement actors (Claeys and Duncan, 2019). Fishers' movements' participation in the IPC and CSM has arguably been crucial in connecting their struggles with those of agrarian, environmental and climate justice movements, amplifying their voices on issues affecting small-scale fishers, and has increased the legitimacy of their demands in the eyes of the intergovernmental organizations.

Fisheries Governance Space: Committee on Fisheries (COFI)

COFI was established in 1965 as a subsidiary body of FAO and is the only international intergovernmental forum that examines fisheries and aquaculture issues at the global level, negotiates agreements and instruments and makes recommendations to governments, regional fisheries bodies, NGOs, fishers and the international community. COFI seeks to supplement, rather than replace, the work of other organizations in the fisheries and aquaculture field. COFI membership is open to all UN Member States, and other

Plenary of the 33rd COFI Session at FAO (Rome), source: author, 2018.

international and regional organizations involved in FAO can participate as observers without voting rights (FAO, 2021b). COFI biennial meetings, which take place at FAO headquarters in Rome, as well as numerous preparatory and sub-committee meetings that take place in between, are exemplary of fisheries governance events in which food security, fish production and climate change mitigation and adaptation are discussed. Alongside formal COFI sessions, many side events take place during the plenary breaks, organized by government delegates in collaboration with FAO, other UN organizations and CSOs (FAO, 2021b).

As of 2021, COFI held 34 official sessions since its first meeting in 1966. Between 1966 and 1975, these sessions were held annually but were switched to biennially in 1977. COFI has established two sub-committees to deal with issues requiring additional technical attention, which meet in the intersessional period between meetings of the full Committee. The Sub-Committee on Fish Trade, established in 1985 to provide a forum to discuss the technical and economic elements of international fish trade as well as relevant elements of production and consumption, held 17 official sessions between 1986 and 2019. Similarly, the Sub-Committee on Aquaculture, established in 2001 as a forum to discuss, consult upon and advise COFI on technical and policy issues related to the aquaculture sector, held 10 sessions between 2002 and 2019. COFI has two main functions: 1) to review FAO's fisheries and aquaculture work programs and their implementation, conduct periodic reviews of international fisheries and aquaculture issues and appraise possible solutions to these issues involving nations, FAO, other intergovernmental bodies and civil society; and 2) to review specific fisheries and aquaculture issues at the request of the Committee, FAO's director-general or the UN General Assembly (FAO, 2021b).

FAO Fisheries Division and Internal Allies

During the last two decades, fishers' movements have built up a long-term relationship with FAO and its Fisheries and Aquaculture Division (NFI). The period since the 2008 Bangkok meeting and the subsequent SSF Guidelines development process has been especially important for strengthening this relationship. NFI defines its vision as "a world in which responsible and sustainable use of fisheries and aquaculture resources makes an appreciable contribution to human well-being, food security and poverty alleviation." In addition, its mission is "to strengthen global governance and the managerial and technical capacities of members and to lead consensus building towards improved conservation and utilization of aquatic resources" (FAO, 2020b). A few NFI staff members have facilitated close collaboration with the fishers' movements. Rolf Willmann, introduced in Chapter 3, was a senior fishery planning officer at FAO who worked on small-scale fisheries issues for 34 years. In a 2013 interview, he described some of the early steps taken to build collaboration between FAO and fishers' organizations:

> Our work depends on intermediaries, and this is why I felt our relationship to civil society organizations is really critical. After I joined [FAO] headquarters in 1982, one of my first tasks was to prepare for a World Conference on Fisheries Management and Development, which was held in 1984. And my concern in the preparations for this conference was always whether small-scale fishing communities and their organizations would be adequately represented in a conference of that nature. So I expressed this concern to my friends in India, the friends I made during my stay there, and they also saw it in this way. So then in 1986, the International Collective in Support of Fishworkers was formed… and the purpose of this organization was really to raise awareness of the role of small-scale fisheries and to support their representatives in decision-making processes and to get wider recognition of this sector. (FAO, 2013)

Willmann and Nicole Franz — who joined FAO in 2011 as a fishery planning analyst and coordinates FAO's support to the implementation of the SSF Guidelines — were central to the Guidelines development process and have been crucial allies to the fishers' movements (FAO, 2014b; TBTI, 2015). They, along with their colleagues in NFI, have been able to support the movements by facilitating access to international spaces and discussions, as well as sharing knowledge on the functioning of intergovernmental UN processes and how to effectively negotiate these processes. Several interviewees commented that Willmann and Franz have also worked closely with fishers' movements and ICSF to ensure small-scale fisheries issues are addressed in COFI agendas and negotiations and have collaborated on countless national and regional projects and workshops focusing on the small-scale sector, addressing issues like secure livelihoods, food security and national level policy (see also FAO, 2014b; FAO, 2013). In a 2014 interview, Franz commented on the crucial role of WFFP and other fishers' organizations in collaborations with FAO:

> In the [SSF Guidelines] implementation process we're looking forward to further supporting organizations like WFFP to work directly with the fishing communities to ensure that the principles that have been integrated and endorsed in the Small-Scale Fisheries Guidelines will actually be transferred to the ground and trigger change on the ground. So we will continue to ensure that WFFP has a chance to gather the voices and the needs of the communities and to bring those views and perspectives and needs up to higher level foras. (FAO, 2014b)

COFI as an Invited and Claimed Space

COFI can be described as an invited space, one in which civil society actors are invited to participate by more powerful actors, which in this case includes intergovernmental bodies and governments. Invited spaces are not simply neutral spaces for participation but are shaped by complex power relations involving relatively powerful and powerless actors (Gaventa, 2006). In some ways, COFI is also a claimed space, which fishers' movements gained access to partially due to their own initiatives and recognition of the importance of having their voices heard in a prominent fisheries governance forum. Their initiatives contributed to strengthening their relationships with key allies within FAO, who recognized the importance of engaging directly with fishers' movements and organizations and who invited them into the COFI space. While critical steps were taken in the 1980s and 90s to build up an alliance between the fishers' movements and FAO, in which Willmann played an important role, this relationship became notably stronger and more consistent after the 2008 Bangkok meeting. Through their strategic engagement in this meeting, the fishers' movements demonstrated why their perspectives are crucial in decision-making processes around global fisheries.

Fishers' movements recognized the advantage of framing their demands in the Bangkok Statement in human rights–based language, a language which has allowed UN organizations like FAO, as well as a wide range of civil society, private sector and governmental organizations, to connect their discourses and find common ground for international collaboration (see Gasper, 2007). As a result, the movements claimed a seat at the table among FAO fisheries officers and researchers from around the world, which contributed to kickstarting the development of the SSF Guidelines and subsequently opened doors for them to participate in COFI. As an organization that worked closely with both FAO and the movements, ICSF was crucial in forging this claimed/invited space, serving as an intermediary in bringing them together. At the same time, allies within FAO, such as Willmann, who already had a long-standing relationship with fishers' movements, supported their participation in FAO's fisheries work and facilitated the opening of institutional doors. These factors in combination have contributed to fishers' movements' active participation in COFI, particularly since 2008, and this participation promises to continue due to COFI's role in the ongoing SSF Guidelines implementation process.

Bringing Fishers' Voices to COFI via the IPC

While some fishers' movement members had been attending COFI sessions in Rome since the early 2000s, movement participation in this space became noticeably more organized, active and visible between 2009 and 2014 during the development of the SSF Guidelines. Since the Guidelines endorsement in 2014, WFFP and WFF have continued to be active in the Guidelines implementation process, both at national and international levels and, in collaboration with FAO and ICSF, have organized numerous side events on the Guidelines process alongside COFI sessions. Fishers' movements participate in COFI sessions as members of the IPC and coordinators of its Fisheries Working Group (Fisheries WG), which is considered the official representative of fishers and fishing communities in COFI. The IPC provides a platform for collaboration between four prominent transnational movements representing constituencies of fishers, farmers, fishers, Indigenous Peoples, fish and agricultural workers, namely WFFP, WFF, LVC and the International Indian Treaty Council (IITC).[1] It provides a common space for mobilization around food sovereignty, linking local and national struggles to global spheres of debate, and facilitates food producer constituencies' participation in transnational food policy processes (Brem-Wilson, 2015).

The IPC is a prominent example of a created autonomous space, emerging from the initiative of social movements seeking a way to have their voices heard at the global level and dissatisfied with the institutionally permitted channels available in the 1990s to participate in global food governance processes. Through the establishment of the IPC, movements were able to define their own structure for participation based on autonomy and self-organization, with representatives from food producing constituencies steering the process, rather than relying on mediated representation, which is often provided by NGOs in global governance processes (Brem-Wilson, 2015). The IPC has been an important convergence space for fishers' movements to interact with like-minded social movements and support NGOs that are challenging corporate control of the global food system and working to develop and promote alternatives from food producers themselves. The space has facilitated discussions between movements that have allowed them to recognize common threats, such as exclusion and marginalization in the food system and the prioritization of industrial agendas that downgrade and undermine the work of small-scale producers. Movements have been able to use the IPC as a channel of communication and interaction to develop collective strategies for addressing these common threats and strengthening and expanding mobilization (Claeys and Duncan, 2019). Fishers' movements' membership in the IPC has been crucial for connecting their struggles to those of agrarian movements, which have comparatively larger membership bases and a wider global reach. In particular, interaction between WFFP, WFF and LVC in the IPC space has created an important channel for knowledge exchange between fishers and farmers, while also helping to amplify fisheries issues through LVC's platforms, statements and demands.

The IPC at the 2018 COFI and the SSF-GSF

In the 33rd COFI Session in 2018,[2] 41 representatives from the IPC Fisheries WG participated. Prior to COFI, the group organized a political workshop and a CSO preparatory meeting, in which the COFI agenda points for engagement were discussed and the IPC strategy was further developed.

An important point of focus for the Fisheries WG during this COFI was the establishment of the Global Strategic Framework in support of the implementation of the SSF Guidelines (SSF-GSF) and the key role of fishers' movements in its Advisory Group. The SSF-GSF is a global mechanism supporting the implementation of the SSF Guidelines at all levels, intended

The IPC Fisheries Working Group pre-COFI preparatory meeting (Rome), source: author, 2018.

to facilitate interactions between COFI members and other interested actors (FAO, 2018c). It was established as the result of discussions and collaboration between the Fisheries WG and FAO, serving as a complementary mechanism for the FAO SSF Umbrella Programme (IPC, 2019b). This program focuses on raising awareness about challenges and opportunities in small-scale fisheries; strengthening the science-policy interface through data collection on the small-scale sector; empowering fishers' organizations; and increasing governments' knowledge, skills and capacity for implementing the SSF Guidelines (FAO, 2021a). At the 2018 COFI, the IPC commented on its role in the SSF-GSF process:

> The SSF-GSF has a central role in the Guidelines implementation process, ensuring to keep the spirit of the Guidelines negotiations and the bottom-up participatory approach as a core principle. IPC is tirelessly working towards SSF Guidelines implementation at grassroots level: we concluded 8 national and 3 sub-regional workshops to raise awareness to our Fisheries communities with the support of IFAD, we are realizing 9 national workshops on Tenure in SSF with the support of FAO, [and] we are discussing with our constituencies and other small-scale fisheries organizations on the priorities for implementation of the Guidelines. (IPC, 2018)

The SSF-GSF Advisory Group includes members of the Fisheries WG — two from WFFP, two from WFF, one from LVC and one from IITC — and is supported by the Office of the United Nations High Commissioner for Human Rights and the International Fund for Agricultural Development (IFAD). The role of the Advisory Group is to promote the coherent and participatory implementation and monitoring of the SSF Guidelines and ensure the process meets international human rights standards. It keeps FAO and COFI informed about the process, facilitates CSO participation and advises the Knowledge Sharing Platform (made up of academia, research institutes and NGOs) and the Friends of the Guidelines (made up of governments members of the COFI) about priorities for the implementation work (see Figure 4.1). In collaboration with global and regional CSOs, the Advisory Group has also played a central role in establishing Regional Advisory Groups in Africa, Asia and the Pacific, and Latin America and the Caribbean. These groups aim to strengthen collaboration among small-scale fishers' organizations and facilitate their participation in SSF Guidelines implementation (IPC, 2019b; FAO, 2018c).

Challenges to Maintaining a Seat at the Table

Movement participation in international spaces involves many challenges, including balancing member organizations' national-level work in addition to international work; dealing with the ebbs and flows in the capacities of

Figure 4.1 SSF-GSF Structure

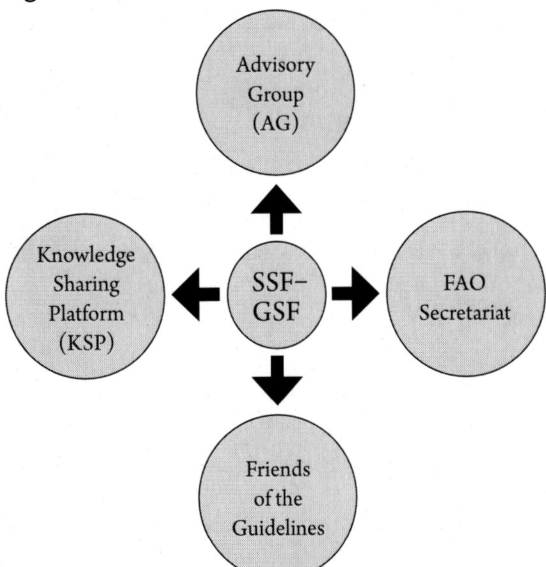

Source: author (using IPC 2019 information)

individuals within those organizations; and framing demands in a language that is acceptable to diverse government actors. As the number of transnational UN and social movement spaces and events have increased since the 1990s, the demands on social movement participation have also increased (Smith, 2013), which in turn "is posing serious challenges to the technical and infrastructural capacities of social movements" (Brem-Wilson, 2015, 84). The unequal power dynamics of such spaces, also pose challenges for movements. Some powerholders in UN committees or government delegations perceive movements solely as observers and do not facilitate their participation in discussions. Some fishers' movement members told me that it is frustrating when the chair of a COFI or CFS session, who decides who gets to speak and when, excludes them. An example of this occurred in a 2012 FAO event; civil society participants walked out of the plenary in response to the chair excluding them from the discussion (see Brem-Wilson, 2015).

While COFI has been an important space for fishers' movements in various ways since the 1980s, even before WFFP and WFF were formally established, it has involved many challenges, particularly during the SSF Guidelines process. Despite playing a central role in this process, fishers' movements members related that they had to make concessions on some of the issues they felt should be included because some governments did not want to make strong commitments toward the universal protection of small-scale fishers' rights and livelihoods. There is also concern among some movement members that since the 2014 endorsement of the Guidelines, their role in the COFI process has become less clear and many governments are not making concerted efforts to implement and uphold the principles of the Guidelines.

The COVID-19 pandemic introduced an additional challenge in that many intergovernmental processes had to be relocated to online platforms, making it even more difficult for civil society representatives to be physically seen and heard in these decision-making spaces and much easier for those in decision-making positions to silence them — sometimes even muting their microphones. Fishers' movements faced this challenge during the virtual 34th COFI Session in 2021, when two days into the plenary agenda, the chair began drastically cutting the time allotted for observer statements. This was reportedly because lengthy discussions (between governments) had led to the schedule being delayed, and by the last few agenda items, observers were no longer able to make statements at all. This effectively silenced civil society participants, who have provided important critical voices in the COFI space. Verbal statements during plenaries are typically the most effective way for civil society representatives to have their voices heard by government delegations, particularly when there is no opportunity to meet in person outside of the sessions. Written statements can be submitted to the Secretariat to be considered, or posted on the COFI website, but there is no way to ensure government delegations or other participants will read these statements. This cutting of time for observer statements was met with a lot of frustration and disappointment from IPC participants, who reflected on the broader trend of shrinking space for social movement voices in intergovernmental spaces and whether this could be a sign of things to come.

The Fisheries WG noted that if COFI were to consider reviewing its process, they "would like to propose that the rules of participation of COFI be reformed to bring them on par with those of modern United Nations institutions like the Committee on World Food Security" (IPC, 2021b). The SSF-GSF Advisory Group further voiced their disappointment:

> We want to express our concern for how the 34th COFI session's modalities are de facto excluding civil society from participation in COFI's proceedings. Efforts have to be made to make COFI a more participatory process and allow civil society members to meaningfully participate in the discussion and decision-making, in line with the principles of participatory governance. This is all the more alarming in light of how the COVID-19 pandemic has severely hit small-scale fisher and Indigenous communities, wherever they may be across the globe. (IPC, 2021b)

Fishers' movements have had to continuously push to have their voices and concerns heard in the COFI space, which first and foremost provides a forum for government delegates to debate fisheries priorities and policies. One movement member told me: "We need to constantly fight for our place at the table, we need to show that we still deserve to be there." Attention to small-scale fisheries has also typically been relatively marginal in COFI, included under a single heading in sessional agendas, in which issues like aquaculture development, fisheries resource management, trade and sustainable development take priority (see, for example, FAO, 2021c, 2018d). To address these challenges, particularly in the post-Guidelines endorsement period, movements have been focusing on how to secure their continued role in the COFI space, such as through active participation and making powerful statements in COFI sessions. Their role in the Advisory Group of the SSF-GSF has also been crucial in order to continue to be centrally involved in the implementation and monitoring of the Guidelines and ensure the process is not co-opted by competing interests.

Food Governance Space: Committee on World Food Security

The Committee on World Food Security (CFS) was established in 1974 as an international intergovernmental forum for reviewing and following up on policies related to the production of and access to food globally. The CFS structure includes the Bureau, Secretariat, Advisory Group and Plenary, comprised of members, participants and observers. Unlike COFI, CFS Sessions are held annually. The Bureau, which is elected by the Plenary every two years and serves as the executive branch of CFS, includes a chair and twelve member countries — two each from Africa, Asia, Europe, the Near East and Latin America, plus one each from North America and Southwest Pacific. The operational functions of CFS are handled by the permanent Secretariat, which supports the Plenary, Bureau and Advisory Group, includes staff from FAO, the International Fund for Agricultural Development (IFAD) and World Food Programme (WFP), and is based at FAO headquarters in Rome. CFS membership is open to all UN Member States, and as of 2021, CFS included 124 states. Participants include representatives from other UN agencies, civil society, NGOs and international agricultural research networks, international and regional financial institutions and private sector associations, while observers can be from other invited organizations with an interest in particular CFS agenda items or programs of work. The Advisory Group is made up of representatives from different categories of participants. This structure was established to allow inputs from stakeholders at national, regional and international levels (FAO, 2021d).

In 2009, CFS went through a reform necessitated by the 2007–08 food price crisis and the subsequent financial crisis that led to rising levels of structural poverty and hunger globally. These crises illuminated the shortcomings of the dominant neoliberal approach to global food governance and policymaking and "opened up a window of political opportunity for change that the food sovereignty movement was ready to seize thanks to a decade of networking and capacity building" (McKeon, 2017b, 77). They also revealed a global governance vacuum in which the absence of democratic authority on global food security had caused decisions in this critical sphere to be taken by default by institutions such as the WTO and World Bank, whose official expertise is not food security, "by donor government groups such as the G8, and—worse still—by economic actors, such as corporations and financial speculators subject to no political oversight" (McKeon, 2017b, 78). The food price crisis was the tipping point of a much larger crisis in the global food system, in which effective food governance had become increasingly complicated by multiple overlapping challenges. Andrée et al. argue:

> The instability of the dominant food system, premised on industrial methods and corporate control, is also affected by the political imperative to respond to a complex set of issues, including the challenges resulting from the financialization of food and the volatility of the global market-place, climate change mitigation and adaptation, food access and safety, and diet-related diseases. This state of flux represents a critical historical moment, full of both challenge and opportunity, for social movements organizing around food to build a more sustainable and just world. (2019, 1)

In response to this crisis in the global food system, UN Secretary-General Ban Ki-Moon established the High-Level Task Force on the Global Food Security Crisis, which accepted proposals for addressing the crisis. The selected proposal, submitted by an alliance of G77 governments,[3] FAO and the IPC for Food Sovereignty, was to reform the existing ineffective CFS and focus on policy-led solutions to the causes of global food insecurity. The reform included redefining CFS's role and vision; expanding participation in CFS to bring in more relevant voices, such as from civil society, on food and agriculture policy; adapting its rules and procedures in order to become the main UN platform addressing food security and nutrition; strengthening its local, national and regional connections; and creating the High-Level Panel of Experts (HLPE) to ensure CFS's work is based on structured expertise and hard evidence (FAO, 2009).

Since the reform, CFS has become one of the key global governance and policymaking spaces for movements focusing on food issues and food sovereignty (Claeys and Duncan, 2019). It is based on a multi-stakeholder approach, through which it collaborates with and coordinates diverse stakeholders and develops and endorses policy guidance and recommendations on a wide range of topics related to food security and nutrition. These recommendations are developed using scientific and evidence-based research conducted by HLPE, as well as technical work supported by FAO, IFAD, WFP and the CFS Advisory Group (FAO, 2021d). Annual CFS sessions are held at FAO headquarters in Rome, and alongside the formal plenaries, there are typically several side events organized by government delegations, FAO and other UN organizations, and civil society. The CFS reform was a more transparent and inclusive process than had been the norm in the UN, and the IPC facilitated the participation of social movements and small-scale

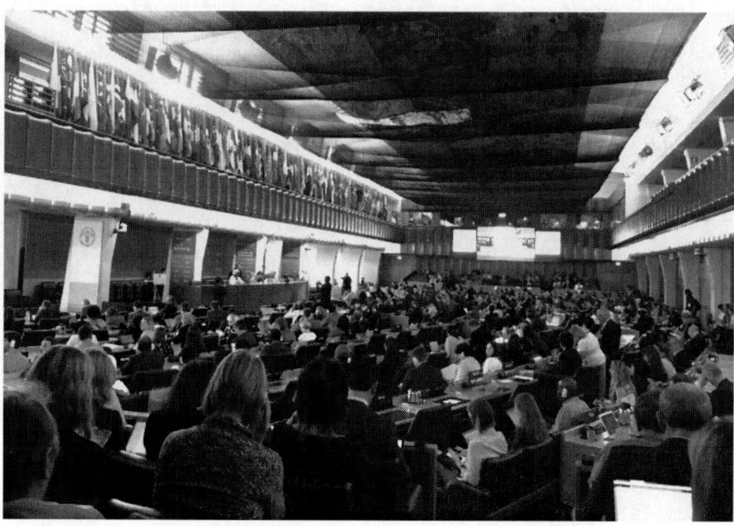

Plenary of the 46th CFS Session at FAO (Rome), source: author, 2019

producers. The resulting CFS, which takes a human rights approach to food and is mandated to coordinate food security policy among a range of institutions globally, is considered the most inclusive global forum dealing with food issues (McKeon, 2017a; Brem-Wilson, 2015).

CFS as an Invited and Claimed Space

Similar to COFI, CFS is arguably a combination of a space which civil society actors have been invited to participate in by (inter)governmental actors and one which civil society has claimed alongside powerful actors, namely governments and intergovernmental agencies (Gaventa, 2006). The role of the IPC in proposing and negotiating the CFS reform alongside the alliance of G77 governments and FAO strategically positioned social movements to help shape an inclusive and participatory CFS space. This role also contributed to strengthening the relationship between the IPC, allied governments and FAO, which ensured that their continued participation in CFS was valued and supported by these allies. A key element of the reform was to establish the International Food Security and Nutrition Civil Society Mechanism for Relations with CFS, which would allow civil society actors to have structural access to CFS and participate directly in CFS plenaries and processes. The CFS reform document states:

> Civil society organizations/NGOs and their networks will be invited to autonomously establish a global mechanism for food

> security and nutrition which will function as a facilitating body for CSO/NGO consultation and participation in the CFS. Such mechanisms will also serve inter-sessional global, regional and national actions in which organizations of those sectors of the population most affected by food insecurity would be accorded priority representation. Civil society organizations/NGOs will submit to the CFS Bureau a proposal regarding how they intend to organize their participation in the CFS in a way that ensures broad and balanced participation by regions and types of organizations. (CFS, 2010, 1)

The proposal to establish a civil society mechanism emerged out of two decades of struggles and advocacy work by movements that were challenging corporate-controlled industrial food systems. The movements had been developing and proposing alternative ways of producing, harvesting, processing, distributing, consuming and even governing food. These alternatives centred around food as a key element of a broader interconnected system in which the health of both people and the environment is crucial and gave more attention to how the food we eat is dependent on the fields, forests, oceans, lakes and rivers that it comes from (Andrée et al., 2019). Through participation in the IPC, movements had been strategizing as to how small-scale food producers themselves could become centrally involved in the food governance processes that directly impacted their lives, and these strategies were key in shaping the proposal for the civil society mechanism. The movements also organized the Peoples' Food Sovereignty Forum, parallel to the World Food Security Summit in 2009, to discuss how they would participate in the newly created civil society space in CFS:

> Civil society has played a fundamentally important role in the CFS reform process, opening up a critical space which we intend to fully occupy in a responsible and effective manner. In so doing, we will ensure that the voices of the excluded continue to be heard at the heart of food and agricultural policy-making and governance, at all levels. (CFS, 2010, 1)

Establishing the Autonomous CSM and Voicing Fishers' Issues

The proposal to include a civil society mechanism was approved as part of the CFS reform, and the CSM was established in 2010. It is the largest international civil society space working toward the eradication of food insecurity and malnutrition. The CSM is a vivid example of a claimed/created space which civil society actors developed autonomously. The structure for the CSM was created during the CFS reform process and involved much debate around how civil society participation was going to be organized and institutionalized within CFS. The resulting CSM was established as an open, inclusive, autonomous body to facilitate civil society participation in CFS discussions and policy processes. The CSM has been an effective space of convergence for diverse social movements to collectively discuss, strengthen and advocate for their alternative vision on global food security and contribute to shaping CFS's work on food policy (Claeys and Duncan, 2019; McKeon, 2017a; Brem-Wilson, 2015). Social movements belonging to constituencies of small-scale farmers or fishers, pastoralists, Indigenous Peoples, agricultural and food workers, landless peoples, women, youth, consumers and urban food insecure, as well as NGOs working on food security and nutrition issues, are free to join and participate in the CSM. Since CFS's reform, hundreds of national, regional and global organizations have participated, with 141 taking part in the 2019 CFS Plenary alone. The CSM has three overarching focuses, including giving priority to organizations and movements representing the people most affected by food insecurity and malnutrition; respecting pluralism, autonomy, diversity and self-organization and trying to ensure there is constituency, gender and regional balance within it; and providing a space for participating organizations to articulate positions and strategies together while freely representing themselves (CSM, 2021; Claeys and Duncan, 2019; FAO, 2019b).

WFFP and WFF both participate in the CSM, although in comparison to COFI, their reach into CFS and the CSM came several years later as fishers' movements had been focusing mostly on the IPC space, which engaged more directly with fisheries issues. Both fishers' movements have members participating in the CSM's Advisory Group and its Coordination Committee (CC), which consists of 41 members from its represented constituencies. The role of the CC is to facilitate civil society activities within their constituencies and sub-regional groups, ensure that the CSM's tasks are carried out effectively and oversee communication processes by sharing information, facilitating consultations and dialogue, and supporting national and regional advocacy and analysis (CSM, 2021). The main difference between the CSM and the IPC is that the CSM is largely funded by CFS and only exists for the purposes of engaging in CFS, while the IPC is largely independent of specific UN or Rome processes. One IPC member I talked with noted that the IPC is a "space for the coming together of social movements, regardless of whether there's a CFS or whether there's a COFI, or whether there's a Human Rights Commission, regardless of any international or UN intergovernmental body, there is IPC." The IPC also supports and is active in the CSM, with IPC members meeting to discuss how they will contribute to the CSM and help with analysis and reflection for developing the CSM's positions within CFS.

Fishers' Movements in the 2019 CFS and CSM Forum

The 46th CFS Session was held in October 2019[4] and included 172 CSOs, 141 of which participated via the CSM — including representatives from WFFP and WFF (FAO, 2019b). The CSM actively participated in the official CFS sessions, making detailed statements responding to agenda items on agroecological approaches, smallholders, the UN Decade on Family Farming, the SDGs and urbanization and rural transformations. The CSM also organized six side events on hunger, human rights and inequalities; the Voluntary Guidelines on Food Systems and Nutrition; re-thinking and re-shaping food systems through agroecology; the impact of extractivism on women's right to food; the future of food and the visions of youth; and the People's Sovereignty Network. Members of the IPC Fisheries WG (from WFFP, WFF and ICSF) also participated in side events on strengthening smallholder food systems and treasures of the oceans and inland waters. This was the first CFS in which the CSM was given a symbolically equal position in the plenary hall, with the CFS chair Mario Arvelo noting during the official opening: "This is the first time we have desegregated the participants in the seating arrangement. CSM representatives are now sitting near the front of the room, rather than at the back." This was an important gesture by the CFS Secretariat, as it demonstrated the value that some CFS members see in the CSM's participation, reflecting not just a top-down gesture but a gradual process of mutual trust-building between CSOs, governments and international organizations.

In the days prior to the 2019 CFS Session, the CSM held its annual forum, in which the CFS agenda was discussed and strategies were developed for effectively engaging in the session, including the establishment of key messages to put forward. This included discussion on political reporting and analysis; the global context of CFS; the HLPE report on agroecology and other innovations; and the *Voluntary Guidelines on Food Systems and Nutrition*. The FAO director general, CFS chair and representatives from IFAD and WFP all spoke in the opening panel of the CSM Forum, highlighting the level of importance CFS places on the CSM. This kind of participation from COFI officials does not occur in the IPC preparatory meetings prior to COFI Sessions.

Some speakers in the CSM Forum mentioned the crucial contributions small-scale fisheries make to the global food system, and several points were raised by representatives from fishers' movements and organizations

Opening Session of the CSM Forum at FAO (Rome), source: author, 2019.

regarding the importance of not leaving fish and fishers out of debates around food security and nutrition. One CSM participant also highlighted that the *Voluntary Guidelines on Food Systems and Nutrition* (VGFSyN), an instrument adopted by CFS at its 47th Session in 2021, does not give adequate attention to fish as an important source of food, with the focus being mainly on crops and agriculture. Situated in a food systems perspective, the VGFSyN is an intergovernmental tool intended for governments and their partners to develop policies and institutional arrangements to address the systemic causes of hunger and malnutrition globally. While the document does mention fishers a handful of times, it mainly refers to fisheries and aquaculture production as a sub-category of agriculture, alongside crops and livestock (see CFS, 2021). Such an approach to fisheries limits the ability of CFS to fully understand and engage with fisheries as a sector that is distinct from farming and requires policy tools that address its specificities in the context of global food systems.

Challenges to Connecting Fisheries and Food Governance

The lack of engagement with fisheries issues in CFS instruments, agendas and sessional reports — despite the CSM including small-scale fishers in its own statements and reports — reflects a broader limitation of CFS: it does not adequately engage with fish as food and a key component of global food security. One fishers' movement interviewee commented:

> CSM will have a fisheries position, but CFS does not. So even though the CSM may make submissions or interventions and mention fisheries, in particular small-scale fisheries, you will never find it

> quoted or repeated within CFS itself… There was a time in 2014 when on the CFS agenda, there was small-scale fisheries as a contributor to food security and nutrition and a resolution was being tabled. There was a "decision box" on small-scale fishing that had to be drafted and prepared, and the Fisheries Working Group of IPC actively took part in that, with the support of the IPC Secretariat, to help structure that decision box.[5]

The marginalization of fishers and fisheries Issues in CFS makes it a difficult space for fishers' movements to engage in as actively as they do in COFI, and some members questioned why they participate. Several members also reflected on how strange it is that two separate intergovernmental spaces exist to deal with food and fisheries, particularly when some of the same national government representatives are present in both CFS and COFI.

Engagement in the CSM is also challenging for fishers' movements because the vast majority of its members come from the agriculture sector. In the 2019 CFS Session and CSM Forum, for example, out of 172 participating civil society organizations, only two were from WFF and WFFP. This imbalance in representation also arguably stems from small-scale farmers receiving significantly more attention in CFS (see also CSM, 2020). This is reflective of a broader issue in global food governance in which fisheries is often treated as a sub-sector of food production, while most attention goes to the role of agriculture in the global food system (Levkoe et al., 2017). While agriculture is a larger sector overall, fisheries provides the primary source of animal protein for 17 percent of the world's population; thus, it plays an integral role in both food security and nutrition (FAO, 2019b). Fishers' movements have attempted to address the marginalization of fisheries issues by building alliances with sympathetic member organizations in the CSM. Along with some other CSM participants, fishers' movements continue to raise the issues faced by small-scale fishers, calling upon both CFS delegates and the CSM to take these issues into account in a more effective way. Yet, it remains to be seen whether fisheries will become a prominent theme in future CFS agendas or reports or in the work of the CSM.

Despite the challenges, many fishers' movements' members told me they still see CFS and the CSM as important spaces for continued engagement, considering their importance in decision-making around global food politics and food system governance. They recognize that these spaces have a major role to play in drawing attention to fisheries issues and ensuring small-scale fishers do not become even further marginalized in food policy discussions. The CSM has also proven to be an effective convergence space for fishers' movements to strengthen their alliances with a broad, diverse network of other civil society actors working on food issues. As a claimed autonomous space, it allows fishers' movements to gain experience participating in a central, structural way in an intergovernmental process, which is not possible to the same degree in COFI due to the external nature of the IPC. Yet, despite the embedded participation that the CSM allows, fishers' movements, in collaboration with their agrarian allies, need to continue to put forward strong, convincing proposals to maintain their legitimacy in CFS, while also focusing on internal capacity-building that both ensures they have articulate spokespersons engaging in the space and that they can expand their roster of leaders with the skills to represent small-scale food producers in global food policy debates (McKeon, 2013).

Climate Governance Space: Conference of the Parties (COP)

The Conference of the Parties (COP) to the United Nations Framework Convention on Climate Change (UNFCCC) (hereafter referred to as COP), first met in Berlin in 1995, following the UNFCCC's 1992 adoption. COP is now the principal international body focusing on national emission limits and climate change mitigation and adaptation goals. Every year, the 197 UNFCCC parties (UN Member States) participate in COP sessions to review the Convention's implementation and related legal instruments and negotiate various institutional and administrative measures intended to improve its implementation. The main task for COP is to review national communications and emission reports submitted by individual parties and assess the effectiveness of the measures being taken and progress being made toward achieving the objectives (UNFCCC, 2021a). The formation of blocs and coalitions are an important element of COP, with many governments grouping together to influence negotiations by extending the reach of their national positions and advancing common agendas. On one side, groups have emerged like the Organization of Petroleum Exporting Countries (OPEC), involving states with strong economic interests in protecting the oil and gas industry and blocking climate change actions. On the other side, the Alliance of Small Island States is a coalition of island states impacted by sea level rise that has proposed some of the most ambitious mitigation targets and plans for reducing emissions (Bulkeley and Newell, 2010). Such competing interests reflect the complexity of the COP space and give an indication of why international climate negotiations have historically been so challenging.

Like COFI and CFS, the structure of COP includes the Bureau and Secretariat. The Bureau, elected from the participating parties, supports COP by providing advice and guidance related to the organization of annual sessions, the operation of the Secretariat and the ongoing work occurring under the UNFCCC, Kyoto Protocol and 2015 Paris Agreement. The Bureau is responsible for managing the COP process and for examining parties' credentials, reviewing the international organizations and NGOs seeking accreditation and compiling regular reports on the process for COP. Meanwhile, the Secretariat, which has been based in Bonn, Germany, since 1996, is responsible for supporting and coordinating the global response to climate change and overseeing emissions reporting (UNFCCC, 2021a). The Secretariat plays a central, yet often underestimated, role in shaping the outcomes of negotiations. While it initially focused on facilitating intergovernmental climate change negotiations, it is now also responsible for providing technical expertise and assistance in analyzing and reviewing the climate change data submitted by the parties (UNFCCC, 2021a; Bulkeley and Newell, 2010). This includes maintaining a publicly accessible database of nationally determined contributions, established under the Paris Agreement, and the plans, policies, targets and actions taken by each participating country toward international climate change mitigation goals (UNFCCC, 2021b).

The annual COP sessions, which are the largest annual UN conferences, take place in a different country each year, unless the designated country is unable to physically host the conference for financial, political or capacity reasons. In such cases, the conference is held in Bonn. The conferences have an average of 25,000 participants, so a host country needs to have substantial infrastructure. The COP presidency alternates between the UN's five regions — Africa, Asia, Central and Eastern Europe, Latin America and the Caribbean, Western Europe and Others. In the last few years, COPs were hosted by France (COP21, 2015); Morocco (COP22, 2016); Germany COP23, 2017); Poland (COP24, 2018); and Spain (COP25, 2019). COP25 was originally planned to be in Chile but had to be relocated due to significant political unrest in the country. COP26, hosted by Scotland in 2021, was postponed from 2020 due to the COVID-19 pandemic (UNFCCC, 2021a).

Annual COP sessions and intersessional meetings have been important moments for mobilizing energy around climate agendas and actions, not only among governments but among a range of civil society actors as well. Due to the high-level nature and scale of COP sessions, the formal conferences are not open to the public and can only be attended by government delegations and accredited organizations. However, CSOs can apply for observer status, and these applications are reviewed and assessed by the

UNFCCC Secretariat to "ensure the coherence and balanced distribution of organizations in line with the constituencies of UNFCCC" (UNFCCC, 2021c). This raises questions about how civil society representatives are selected and what criteria are used to determine if there is coherence and balance among them. Rising international concern about the climate crisis has contributed to a significant increase in CSOs applying to participate in COP, making it increasingly difficult for new applicants to receive accreditation (Orr, 2016). Bulkeley and Newell explain:

> Alongside the formal negotiations organized in plenary sessions and working groups that meet in parallel to discuss specific issues, a bewildering array of non-governmental, business and other organizations are registered to participate in the process. Though they do not have formal voting rights, they are allowed to make interventions and are often admitted into government delegations where they have access to all the meetings taking place. In many ways, these actors are non-governmental "diplomats" that perform many of the same functions as state delegates: representing the interests of their constituencies, engaging in information exchange, negotiating, and providing policy advice. (2010, 19)

Principled Non-Participation and Parallel Climate Justice Space

In contrast to COFI and CFS, in which social movements have been able to participate directly, COP is a more closed space, in which powerful actors — namely governments and intergovernmental organizations — are negotiating and making decisions. This sort of closed space tends not to facilitate the broadening of inclusionary boundaries that would enable direct participation by a wider range of civil society actors. States may consider these to be "provided" spaces in which an elite group of bureaucrats, selected representatives and experts makes decisions and provides services to the broader society, with the view that broader consultation or involvement is not necessary. Some CSOs focus their efforts on trying to pry open these closed spaces by demanding increased participation, more transparency and greater accountability to the public (Gaventa, 2006). While some larger CSOs and NGOs with the capacity have chosen to form alliances with their national governments in order to join delegations and gain access to COP sessions, many civil society representatives remain excluded. Social movements which have a particularly critical perspective on the solutions proposed and the climate mitigation actions being taken by governments are unable to access COP sessions, and some choose not to as a strategy of resistance (Chatterton et al., 2013; Featherstone, 2013). This strategy of "principled non-participation" involves individual actors or groups "opt[ing] out of civic and political activity on the basis of principle" (MacGinty, 2012, 173). MacGinty further explains:

> The principle is one of non-recognition of the legitimacy of international actors, their local proxies and the processes that they institute. As such, it is a political act and can be interpreted as a form of communication at the out-group and in-group levels. It is worth stressing that the agency involved in principled non-participation is reactionary and is a response to an agenda largely set by others. This illustrates the importance of power relations in considerations of non-participation. (2012, 174)

Transnational social movements engaging with issues of climate justice, such as LVC, WFFP, WFF and the International Indigenous Peoples Forum on Climate Change (IIPFCC), take different approaches to engagement with the UNFCCC process. A decade of international advocacy led by Indigenous movements to include Indigenous Peoples' rights in the Convention resulted in IIPFCC being officially recognized in 2008 as a UNFCCC constituency able to represent Indigenous Peoples in COPS. IIPFCC's contributions have centred around regaining control over ancestral territories and ensuring that their rights to land and natural resources are protected in the development of climate-related actions (Claeys and Delgado Pugley, 2017; Chatterton et al., 2013).

In contrast, LVC has chosen not to participate in COPS but has contributed to the organization of parallel civil society events promoting climate justice, using intergovernmental climate discussions to "advance their alternative development paradigm grounded in food sovereignty, agroecology and peasants' rights" (Claeys and Delgado Pugley, 2017, 326). Their strategy of principled non-participation in the COP space reflects their fundamental disagreement with what they call "false solutions" to climate change — referring to initiatives such as agrofuel production, carbon trading, REDD+ (reducing emissions from deforestation and forest degradation) and climate-smart agriculture, forestry and fisheries (CSA).[6] Such initiatives, which are heavily influenced by corporate interests, promote technological and market-driven solutions to climate change rather than addressing the structural political and economic issues that are contributing to environmental degradation and marginalizing those most affected. On the other hand, the climate justice movement, which calls for "system change, not climate change," highlights how climate change is disproportionally affecting food-producing and Indigenous communities and promotes solutions put forward by these communities as a way to achieve a just transition for both people and the environment (Clapp et al., 2018; Claeys and Delgado Pugley, 2017; Tramel, 2016; Martinez-Alier et al., 2016; LVC, 2007).

Similarly, WFFP and WFF rejected the "false climate solutions" proposed by governments, while also employing a strategy of principled non-participation in the COP space. Thus, their engagement with COP does not take the same direct form that it does with COFI and CFS and focuses instead on parallel civil society spaces aimed at promoting alternatives like food sovereignty, agroecology and climate justice, while following some UNFCCC processes virtually. Fishers' movements have been engaging with issues emerging from the climate crisis, including impacts on fishing communities and the effects of mitigation and adaptation initiatives on small-scale fisheries, internalizing these issues in their agendas and political strategies. Part of their strategy has been to strengthen alliances with movements such as LVC that are struggling for climate justice and promoting the positive contributions made by small-scale fishers and farmers to mitigating climate change through sustainable and responsible approaches to food production. A key part of this alliance-building process involved mobilization around COP21 in Paris in 2015. As Tramel notes, this involved a

> collective transnational process rooted in local experience that intentionally featured marginalized voices spanning the global South and North, among them, women, rural peasants, urban migrants, indigenous peoples, and low-income communities of color. It is through these kinds of dialogues and maximization of scarce resources that people are figuring out together how to fight back against what they consider false solutions to climate change proposed by corporations and governments. (2016, 2)

COP21 and the Zone of Action for the Climate

COP21 was a momentous event in which parties came together to negotiate the Paris Agreement, a document focusing on strengthening state-level responses to tackling climate change, efforts to limit the temperature increase to 1.5 degrees above pre-industrial levels and setting targets for national contributions to climate mitigation (UN, 2015b). There was a huge amount of international energy and attention built up around COP21 due to the expectation that, for the first time in history, an agreement would be established uniting all parties in their commitment to undertake ambitious efforts

Zone of Action for the Climate (Paris), source: author, 2015.

to combat climate change and adapt to its impacts. The Paris Agreement, however, turned out to be a disappointment for social movements, such as LVC, WFFP and WFF, fighting for human rights as the text only mentions human rights once in its preamble, noting that "parties should, when taking action to address climate change, respect, promote and consider their respective obligations on human rights" (UN, 2015b, 2). The agreement is particularly troublesome considering it does not put forward any legally binding obligations for parties to frame their climate actions in a human rights–based approach (Claeys and Delgao Pugley, 2017).

Parallel to the official COP, there were critical gains made for social movements in terms of transnational mobilization and alliance-building. In another area of Paris, social movements organized the parallel Zone of Action for the Climate (ZAC), in which hundreds of CSOs, including LVC, WFFP and WFF, held meetings and workshops to debate the false solutions to climate change being promoted by world leaders. ZAC was a vibrant example of a space created autonomously by civil society actors to lead their own climate summit. During ZAC, fishers, farmers, pastoralists and social movement representatives discussed the effectiveness of the climate solutions being presented by world leaders and put forward alternative approaches and "real solutions" to protect the environment and climate (Mills, 2018). Declarations, statements and reports reflecting these discussions were written and shared widely online (see LVC, 2015a; LVC, 2015b; WFFP, 2015a; WFFP, 2015c). A WFFP report argued for real solutions to climate change that included respecting and not exploiting nature; acknowledging traditional and Indigenous knowledge; democratic governance and community-driven natural resource management; and prioritizing human rights over corporate rights. The report discussed ways to pursue climate justice, including building alliances and converging with other movements; mass mobilization; the central role of women in leading local struggles; taking legal action against governments and companies for infringement of human rights; and making use of human rights and UN instruments (WFFP, 2015a).

At ZAC, WFFP and WFF co-organized a meeting called "Blue Carbon: Ocean Grabbing in Disguise?" to discuss the blue carbon mechanism of UNFCCC. This mechanism involves selling credits for carbon sequestered in coastal mangroves, tidal marshes and seagrasses (Thomas, 2014). The movements argued that carbon credits perpetuate a politico-economic system that profits from the commodification of nature. This event also argued that fisher peoples' control of water and land is a crucial element of climate justice. Despite being from many different regions and national fishers' organizations, all the speakers shared a common concern for the impact such agendas could have on fishing communities and a common vision for alternative strategies to protect coastal environments (WFFP, 2015c; Mills, 2018; Damanik, 2015). The workshop report notes that "blue carbon needs to be understood as part of broader processes of the privatisation of nature

Civil Society Climate Justice March (Paris, 2015), source: author.

and grabbing resources under the guise of conservation" (WFFP, 2015a, 1). One WFFP member commented: "In Indonesia, the fishers say, 'the sea is our mother who provides, protects and loves us.' The blue carbon project asks us to sell our mother" (WFFP, 2015a, 3). WFF and WFFP members also participated in the Global Convergence of Land and Water Struggles, an initiative launched a few months earlier with representatives from frontline communities around the world to discuss the transformation of the global food system. The participants argued for the realization of food systems based on food sovereignty and agroecology models, centred on small-scale food producers' access to and control over land and natural resources. The culmination of the week-long ZAC was a massive demonstration in which 30,000 people, including members of WFFP and WFF, marched across Paris demanding climate and social justice (Mills, 2018; Tramel 2016; LVC, 2015a).

COP Complexity and Limits to Movement Capacity

The complexity of the COP space, and broader climate politics that it contributes to, present numerous challenges for social movement participation. As mentioned above, the formation of government blocs and coalitions among UNFCCC parties, some of which involve powerful economic interests like agribusiness, financial institutions and the oil and gas industry, make power imbalances within climate politics difficult for movements to navigate (Bulkeley and Newell, 2010; Chatterton et al., 2013; Featherstone, 2013). Newell argues:

> The terrain of climate politics shifts rapidly, and policy arenas such as the nation-state, where decisions were traditionally made, become less and less relevant. Instead, policy action on climate change resides in a plurality of private and public, formal and informal sites of regulation. This altered framework of governance in itself creates accountability challenges, given that traditional channels of representation and participation often do not exist in private and non-state spheres, and rights to information and consultations are not easily applied to private sectors. (2011, 225)

The COP space has had a history of restricting civil society participation, with one particularly controversial example being COP15 in 2009 in Copenhagen, where the Copenhagen Accord was negotiated. Although 13,500 civil society observers had been allowed to register, the conference organizers decided at the last minute that only 1,000 participants would be permitted inside on the second-last day of the meeting, further decreasing this number to 90 on the final day. Civil society actors responded with a mix of anger and disappointment. COP21 in Paris introduced restrictive limits on civil society participation from the start, allowing organizations just two to five slots for their representatives (Orr, 2016). This decision may have contributed to the large number of CSOs that decided to join the parallel ZAC space.

Although energy leading up to and during COP21 was vibrant, fishers' movements' engagement with COP has decreased since 2015, with only a few representatives able to participate in a social movement–led climate justice training organized in Morocco parallel to the 2016 COP22. For the four most recent COPs, in Germany (2017), Poland (2018), Spain (2019) and Scotland (2021), livestreaming of the events allowed more virtual participation globally, and some fishers' movement members were able to follow the processes online. However, online participation can be an obstacle for the many movement members who live and work in remote areas and have limited access to the internet. Virtual meetings may also pose challenges for ensuring inclusivity and transparency in the proceedings, which is best achieved in in-person settings. An additional obstacle arose in 2019 when COP25 had to be relocated to Spain just a few weeks before the conference due to political unrest in Chile, making it difficult for CSOs to quickly shift their organizational capacities to Madrid and mobilize as strongly as they had originally planned. There were many logistical reasons for the lack of physical participation by fishers' movements in the four recent COPs, including lack of travel funds and the complicated process of getting European visas. However, there are also more structural capacity issues which prevent fishers' movements from participating in international climate processes. One movement member told me:

> I don't think that the movements are necessarily strong enough to have a presence in all climate spaces or moments when they arise. I think a lot depends on the strength of the alternative movement or organizations in that country. It just so happened that in Paris, there was quite a strong movement that was in opposition to the mainstream climate agenda, and would in fact, argue an alternative worldview than what is being discussed on the [COP plenary] floor. That's what I understand was the strength in Paris … It is the strength of the political agenda of the progressives in that country that will make it happen. But if we don't have a presence, either through members, or through a local organization there, it's not

> likely to happen. We don't have the resources to go there from outside [the country]. Capacity-wise it's just not possible.

Thus, the location of member organizations is an important factor in the participation of fishers' movements in climate spaces parallel to COPs. While COPs 23, 24 and 26 took place in countries where WFFP and WFF do not have members (Germany, Poland and Scotland), COP25 was in Spain, where WFFP has a member. As mentioned above, this made it difficult to quickly organize a large international civil society event involving participants from outside of Europe — particularly for movements like WFFP and WFF, with members largely based in the Global South and with limited financial and human resources for international travel.

Considering that COP is the key space for determining international climate regulations, by which small-scale fishers' livelihoods and survival are directly impacted, not having the capacity to participate in parallel civil society spaces is a big loss for transnational fishers' movements. It is important for them to continue to devote time and energy to ensuring that their voices are not left out of climate discussions and that they do not lose what little ground small-scale fishers have gained in climate spaces over the last two decades. Since climate politics is a relatively new sphere for fishers' movements, a significant amount of energy will need to be devoted to capacity-building so members are better equipped to engage in climate-related spaces and debates. This also involves being prepared for the waves of activity and energy that typically characterize social movements and ensuring that leaders are able to guide members through ebbs and flows in mobilization. One movement member said:

> It's typical of how social activism works. There are moments of heightened activity or activism, and there are moments where it is less so. It depends entirely on the leadership that we have, the strength or the nature of the issue that drives the political agenda or the developmental agenda. And it depends on capacities and how interested people are. Not just people who are immersed in the issue, but the broader solidarity movement you have in the world. The strength of the solidarity movement can also act as an energizer for local conditions and for local struggle. But struggles like the climate crisis is a global struggle. It's not just a developing country issue.

Despite the many challenges to participation, international climate spaces and processes, such as COP, are crucial for fishers' movements, which often point out that the "effects of climate change on the coastline will hit small-scale fishers first, because they operate in the near shore, and if the conditions there change, they can't go into the deep, they don't have the means." Civil society–led climate justice spaces are also crucial because they reflect a common thread linking fisheries, agrarian and climate justice initiatives, with spaces such as ZAC marking important moments for convergence between transnational fishers', agrarian and climate movements. The creation of these shared international spaces has allowed civil society actors from once separate arenas to discuss and better understand each other's narratives and find ways to engage with them collectively. These spaces have made crucial contributions to both alliance-building and expanding and broadening the scope of transnational fishers' and agrarian movements. These alliances are hinged upon food production as a central issue in climate change debates, with movements calling into question the current destructive modes of production, circulation and consumption. Together, these movements are illuminating their common struggle for access to and control over resources, stemming from simultaneous threats of climate change and mitigation and adaptation initiatives, and combining their efforts as a strategy for extending their international reach (Mills, 2018).

Concluding Remarks

Exploring the international spaces that fishers' movements are prioritizing provides important insights into the strategies they are using to contest and influence fisheries, food and climate politics. As a central focus for movements' political energy, participation in COFI has been possible as the result of two key factors: first, through the movements' own political initiative and capacities, they recognized the importance of intergovernmental UN spaces for their struggles, while also understanding the power of the human rights framework prominent in UN agendas. Targeting FAO spaces and framing their demands firmly in relation to the human rights of small-scale fishers, such as in the 2008 Bangkok Statement, proved to be an effective strategy for scaling up their struggles onto international platforms. Second, key allies within FAO committed to engaging directly with fishers' movements and fishing communities have been crucial in opening COFI doors, particularly after the Bangkok meeting and the subsequent SSF Guidelines development process. The post-Guidelines endorsement period has posed some important challenges for the movements in maintaining mobilization at the international level, particularly as members shift their focus to national-level implementation. However, the active participation of committed IPC Fisheries Working Group members and their role in the Advisory Group of the SSF-GSF has secured movements' continued involvement in the implementation of the Guidelines.

CFS has been a more challenging space for fishers' movements' engagement due to its prioritization of agriculture and lack of attention to fisheries. Despite the challenges, there have been three important outcomes of fishers' movements' engagement in CFS. First, as the most participatory intergovernmental space dealing with food issues, CFS and its CSM have provided a channel for fishers' movements to participate directly in a high-level UN process. This has contributed to expanding their international experience, strengthening their political analysis and capacity, and increasing their visibility within FAO. Second, the CSM has become a crucial convergence space for fishers' and agrarian movements, which has bolstered their alliances, enhanced their collective agendas and strategies, and expanded agrarian movements' engagement with fisheries issues, and vice versa. Third, fishers' movements have consistently brought fish to the (food) table in CFS and the CSM by highlighting small-scale fishers' issues and the importance of fish for global food security and nutrition. This has been crucial for raising the profile of fisheries issues in these spaces and for expanding the food governance agenda beyond agriculture, crops and livestock.

Engagement with COP has illuminated a different form of participation from the COFI and CFS spaces. Rather than participating directly in COP, fishers' movements have focused on contributing to autonomous spaces that challenge the false solutions proposed by governmental institutions and corporate partners. Their participation in these spaces has had two important outcomes. First, climate justice spaces like ZAC in Paris and CSO training in Morocco have been crucial convergence spaces for fishers', agrarian and climate movements, offering moments for strategy discussions, capacity-building and deepening mutual understandings between movements engaging in the global climate justice movement. Second, these interactions with movements with a longer history of climate justice engagement have been important for enhancing fishers' movements' understanding and analysis of climate politics. This has strengthened their capacity to engage with global climate debates and address the disproportionate impacts of climate change on small-scale fishing communities in their advocacy work. Agrarian and climate movements have also been able to learn more about the impacts of climate change and mitigation and adaptation initiatives on small-scale fishers and engage with these issues in their own work.

Fishers' movements have made important contributions to COFI, CFS and COP spaces by voicing the concerns of small-scale fishers and advocating for the human rights and livelihoods of fishers to be respected and protected. Their role in these spaces has been to provide a critical voice, raising questions about mainstream approaches and agendas and offering alternatives that take into account the knowledge and experience of fishers and fishing communities. While human, knowledge and financial capacities have limited their engagement with many important international spaces, they continue to work on maintaining space for themselves in COFI, CFS and COP, recognizing these as crucial for their struggles. Some ground has been lost while other ground has been gained, and mobilization and active participation have ebbed and flowed over time. Yet, fishers' movements have managed to make themselves visible in international platforms and debates situated within a global context that does not prioritize small-scale fishers. Without their advocacy and collaborations with key allies, the human rights of small-scale fishers and their crucial contributions to the global food system and environmental protection would have slipped even further off the radar.

NOTES

1. IITC is an organization of Indigenous Peoples from North, Central, South America, the Caribbean and the Pacific working for the sovereignty and self-determination of Indigenous Peoples.
2. The 34th COFI Session, which was postponed from July 2020 due to the COVID-19 pandemic, was held online in February 2021. The 35th COFI session, which was organized as a hybrid event in September 2022, took place after this book was completed.
3. The G77 is a coalition of 134 governments from the Global South which promotes its members' collective economic interests and enhances their joint negotiating capacity within the UN.
4. The 47th, 48th and 49th CFS sessions were held online in 2021 due to the COVID-19 pandemic. The 50th session is being organized as a hybrid event in October 2022.
5. CFS (2014) published a policy report entitled *Sustainable Fisheries and Aquaculture for Food Security and Nutrition,* including nine recommendations, the first of which is to "give to fish the position it deserves in food security and nutrition strategies, policies and programmes."
6. REDD+ is a framework created by COP "to guide activities in the forest sector that reduce emissions from deforestation and forest degradation, as well as the sustainable management of forests and the conservation and enhancement of forest carbon stocks in developing countries" (UNFCCC, 2021d). CSA is an approach for developing agricultural strategies oriented toward ensuring food security in the context of climate change. It focuses on "sustainably increasing agricultural productivity and incomes; adapting and building resilience to climate change; and reducing and/or removing greenhouse gas emissions, where possible" (FAO, 2021e).

5 Contentious Fisheries Issues

At the Heart of Social and Political Struggles

Global fisheries have become increasingly complicated by intersections with food and climate crises, as well as rural and environmental transformations. While discussions on such transformations tend to focus on agriculture and land, particularly in the context of agrarian political economy and critical agrarian studies, useful insights into the causes and consequences of changing global contexts can be gained from fisheries (Campling and Colás, 2021; Campling et al., 2012; Sundar, 2012). The impacts rural and environmental transformations have on fishers and fishing communities globally confirm the importance of fishers' movements organizing beyond national boundaries and expanding internationally. These movements have responded to global shifts in a variety of ways, including in the political agendas they establish, the issues they highlight, the actions they engage in and the spaces they participate in.

Fishers' movements have been shaping their political agendas and making demands around contentious issues since the 1990s, particularly in relation to the exclusion and dispossession of small-scale fishers from traditional fishing areas and resources. Through their participation in the IPC Fisheries WG, the movements have called attention to issues related to the impacts of the blue economy and blue growth agendas, ocean and coastal grabbing, industrial aquaculture expansion, the neglect of inland fisheries and the loss of aquatic genetic resources and biodiversity (IPC, 2019b). These issues emerge from a global context — shaped by overlapping waves of development — in which capital is continuously expanding through privatization and corporate agendas, facilitating uneven development in fisheries (O'Connor, 1998; Campling and Colás, 2021). Subsequent social, political and economic obstacles have undermined small-scale fisheries and shaped how movements frame their narrative and reactions. Their narrative reflects an anti-capitalist character, focusing on multiple layers of injustice, which is central to the development of a "powerful counter-hegemonic project of eco-societal transformation" (Fraser, 2021, 97). This narrative and its core issues are explored in this chapter.

IPC Fisheries Working Group

The IPC's five working groups, which focus on agricultural biodiversity; agroecology; fisheries; Indigenous Peoples; and land, forests, water and territory, were established in 2013 as part of a strategic decision to engage more explicitly with the issues at the core of the IPC's work. The focus of most of these groups can be directly linked to LVC's main thematic issues, which include agrarian reform, food sovereignty and trade, agroecology, biodiversity and genetic resources, human rights, women and gender, and youth (LVC, 2021; Edelman and Borras, 2016; Rosset, 2013). The Fisheries WG, however, has largely been the domain of the fishers' movements, with representatives from LVC and IITC only recently beginning to play a more active role. It is the main international space for civil society coordination and collaboration on fisheries issues and includes representatives from WFFP, WFF and support NGOs, namely Crocevia (IPC Secretariat), ICSF, TNI and FIAN (IPC, 2019a).[1]

In 2014, shortly after the endorsement of the SSF Guidelines, fishers' movements began scaling up the work of the Fisheries WG as part of a strategic decision to expand and concretize their focus on food sovereignty, which is at the core of the IPC's work. This strategic shift has involved campaigning for the realization of food sovereignty in local fisheries contexts, strengthening their alliances with other social movements working toward similar goals and advocating for the SSF Guidelines (KNTI and WFFP, 2017).

> Through the space of alliance and coordination offered by the IPC Working Group on Fisheries, the major global civil society networks representing small-scale fisheries have joined together to bring the voice of their communities to international political decision-making bodies. This advocacy work has made it possible to achieve one of the main achievements of the IPC when, in 2014, the [SSF Guidelines] were endorsed by the FAO Committee on Fisheries (COFI). The key role played by the IPC in developing the SSF Guidelines was acknowledged by COFI when, two years later,

> with the establishment of the FAO SSF Umbrella Programme and the Global Strategic Framework in support of the implementation of the SSF Guidelines (SSF-GSF), the IPC Working Group on Fisheries was identified to act as the SSF-GSF Advisory Group. (IPC, 2019b)

Through their participation in numerous events, meetings, webinars and workshops, the Fisheries WG has played an important role in guiding how fishers' movements engage with and are represented in COFI and CFS and in shaping movement discourse in international civil society and research spaces. As well as providing critical analysis on and responding to contentious issues, the group has also been crucial in moving the SSF Guidelines implementation process forward.

Transnational fishers' movements and allied organizations have collectively identified several crosscutting issues that are central to their struggles and require critical analysis. These issues, including blue economy, ocean grabbing, aquaculture, aquatic genetic resources and inland fisheries, have been at the centre of the Fisheries WG's advocacy work and prominent in its statements and demands since 2014. The blue economy agenda, ocean grabbing processes and aquaculture expansion reflect interests competing for aquatic spaces that small-scale fishers depend on for their livelihoods and pose urgent threats to the survival of the small-scale sector. The preservation of aquatic genetic resources is central to ensuring the longevity of small-scale fisheries, which are dependent on biodiversity and healthy, well-balanced aquatic ecosystems, particularly in shallow coastal areas. Attention to inland fisheries has also become an important issue for fishers' movements in the last few years, due to concern that there was an imbalanced focus in international fisheries governance on marine fisheries and spaces, despite millions of people around the world depending on inland lakes and rivers for fishing livelihoods (IPC, 2019b; WFFP, 2017. These issues and concrete examples of how fishers' movements are engaging with them are explored in the following sections.

Exclusionary Blue Economy and Blue Growth Agendas

The "blue economy" concept and agenda first appeared at the UN's 2012 Conference on Sustainable Development (more commonly known as Rio+20), in which ocean issues and governance were discussed and negotiated. This unprecedented attention to the oceans was sparked by global concern about overfishing, marine biodiversity loss, climate change–induced ocean temperature rise and acidification, and a growing consensus among governments about the urgency to prioritize the conservation and sustainable development of the oceans (Silver et al., 2015). The blue economy essentially encompasses all economic activities in the oceans, framing marine resources as key for addressing global challenges such as food security, climate change and the provision of renewable energy. The breadth of its scope has unsurprisingly meant that a vast array of actors is driving the agenda, many of which have competing perspectives. Many others — namely small-scale fishers — find themselves completely excluded from the development of initiatives that promise to have serious impacts on their livelihoods (Mallin et al., 2019).

As a development agenda, the blue economy has been promoted particularly vigorously by governments in Europe and small island developing states (SIDS), such as Fiji, Saint Lucia, Mauritius and Seychelles, which are on the frontlines of climate impacts and have maritime sectors that play a significant role in their national economies (Bennett et al., 2019; Silver et al., 2015). The blue economy agenda claims to simultaneously generate wealth and conserve ocean biodiversity through market-based approaches to conservation and mechanisms that place value on resource sustainability (Charles et al., 2014). This agenda promises win-win-win solutions in which coastal communities, the environment and investors can all benefit, while failing to acknowledge the contradictions that exist between continuously chasing economic growth and conserving and restoring ocean resources as an approach to mitigating climate change (Mallin and Barbesgaard, 2020; Barbesgaard, 2018).

In 2015, international interest in the blue economy grew exponentially, with a flood of conferences on investment in the blue economy and ways to achieve "blue growth" being organized and funded by governments, environmental NGOs, conservation organizations, financial institutions and military companies. The European Commission, which had adopted its own blue growth strategy in 2012, positioned blue growth at the centre of its maritime contribution to the Europe 2020 Strategy for smart, sustainable and inclusive growth (European Parliament, 2020; Mallin and Barbesgaard, 2020). The reach of both the blue economy and blue growth extend well beyond the fisheries sector, encapsulating the management of all maritime and coastal resources. Silver et al. (2015) pinpoint four broad discourses in which the blue economy is being employed, including oceans as natural capital, good business, integral to SIDS and integral to small-scale fisheries livelihoods. In relation to the last category, which is particularly relevant here, the increasing prominence of "blue" agendas poses a serious threat to fisheries sectors globally by competing for aquatic resources and spaces, squeezing out fishing activities in favour of more lucrative aquatic investments, such as deep-sea mining, ecotourism and offshore energy (Bennett et al., 2021; Barbesgaard, 2018; Eikeset et al., 2018).

Small-scale fishers and coastal communities stand to be the hardest hit by the increasing number of initiatives popping up under the pretext of blue economy development, as many of the coastal areas targeted by "blue investors" are those in which small-scale fishers live and depend on for their livelihoods. These areas end up being closed off to fishing activities in favour of coastal industries and resource conservation. Examples of this include marine protected areas (MPAs) and blue carbon credits. While both initiatives were part of marine conservation agendas before the emergence of the blue economy agenda, with the first MPAs being established in the 1970s and blue carbon's role in "healthy oceans" being discussed in a prominent 2009 report (see Nellemann et al., 2009), they have been drawn into and promoted as part of the blue economy discourse (Silver et al., 2015; Barbesgaard, 2018; Thomas, 2014).

The creation of some protected areas can be understood as what Wolff calls "protectionist, authoritarian and violently repressive practice of conservation" that have caused people to lose "their rights of access to vast areas of the most productive marine resource sites, which they consider themselves to have traditionally governed and utilized sustainably in the past" (2015, 16). Bennett et al. (2021) specify ten social injustices that can be produced by blue growth agendas: 1) dispossession, displacement and ocean grabbing; 2) environmental justice concerns from pollution and waste; 3) environmental degradation and reduction of ecosystem services; 4) livelihood impacts for small-scale fishers; 5) lost access to marine resources needed for food security and well-being; 6) inequitable distribution of economic benefits; 7) social and cultural impacts of ocean development; 8) marginalization of women; 9) human and Indigenous rights abuses; and 10) exclusion from decision-making and governance.

Fishers' movements have been responding to these injustices, criticizing blue economy and blue growth agendas and speaking out about various initiatives, particularly since international interest in these agendas were ramped up in 2015. They criticize the fact that blue agendas have had little, if any, engagement with small-scale fishers' organizations and movements, while presenting a vision for a sustainable future that leaves little space for the survival of small-scale fisheries. The Fisheries WG argues:

> Seen as the formula for combining food production, environmental protection and economic gain, the so-called "blue economy"

> refers to a series of economic practices that try to integrate the exploitation of natural resources with the preservation of local ecosystems. Nevertheless, this solution fails to address the main problems related to the capitalistic management of maritime resources, feeding the illusion of a green — blue in the present case — growth. Moreover, the development of this economic paradigm, and the practices it contains, has been done without the participation, or even the consultation, of small-scale fisheries communities. Their ancestral knowledge is not valorized, nor are their traditions and their spiritual link with the ecosystems they are part of, both sacrificed to the altar of the economic gain. (IPC, 2019b)

In terms of activities, fishers' movements have held workshops and released numerous public statements and publications, stressing that the win-win-win promises of blue agendas are false and actually stand to marginalize small-scale fishers even further by separating them from fishing resources and areas. As mentioned in Chapter 4, the fishers' movements organized a workshop in 2015 parallel to COP21 framing blue carbon as ocean grabbing in disguise and a false solution to climate change. A public statement was also released in which fishers' movements argued that this "so-called protection does more harm than good. The way actors pushing blue carbon envision 'conservation' will result in the displacement of people who live off and with these areas. Their brand of conservation involves expulsion of communities, reducing customary or community access rights and fundamentally changing communities' relationship with resources" (WFFP and WFF, 2015a).

Movement members have also participated in "blue justice" workshops, meetings and webinars. Blue justice, a concept introduced by Moenieba Isaacs in 2018, is a social justice–centred response to blue economy and blue growth debates, which was later expanded into a campaign by the research network Too Big to Ignore (TBTI)[2] (Isaacs, 2019). TBTI explains blue justice as "a critical examination of how coastal communities and small-scale fisheries may be affected by blue economy and blue growth initiatives that promote sustainable ocean development but neglect SSF and their contribution to ocean sustainability" (2019). This debate is relatively new and still developing, and it is yet to be seen whether blue justice initiatives will have concrete, material impacts in the lives of small-scale fishers. However, fishers' movements continue to keep a critical eye on the evolving blue discourses and agendas, demanding that the rights and livelihoods of small-scale fishers be protected and that such initiatives do not perpetuate ocean and coastal grabbing.

Dispossession and Displacement Caused by Ocean and Coastal Grabbing

The rise of the blue economy and blue growth reflects the continued expansion and latest phase of broader global processes of ocean and coastal grabbing. Both involve similar processes and impacts to those of land grabbing, a phenomenon that has been spurred by converging food, energy, financial and environmental crises (Borras and Franco, 2012). The ocean grabbing narrative highlights processes and dynamics that negatively affect people small-scale fishers and coastal communities, whose lives and livelihoods depend on fisheries and coastal resources. The fishers' movements and several allied organizations define ocean grabbing as "the capturing of control by powerful economic actors of crucial decision-making around fisheries, including the power to decide how and for what purposes marine resources are used, conserved and managed now and in the future" (TNI, 2014, 3). It has been described as "dispossession or appropriation of use, control or access to ocean space or resources from prior resource users, rights holders or inhabitants" (Bennett et al., 2015, 62). It can be perpetuated by both private interests and public institutions, occurring via inappropriate governance processes, and may involve actions that impact human security, livelihoods or social-ecological well-being (Bennett et al., 2015).

The result is that powerful actors, such as corporations and financial institutions, take control of fisheries resources in the interest of profiting from them, while small-scale fishers and coastal communities lose access. This enclosure of resources is mainly facilitated through laws, policies and practices that prioritize private ownership and management without taking into account the damaging social and environmental impacts. More specifically, it occurs through a variety of mechanisms, such as national and international fisheries governance and energy policies; the establishment of conservation areas; ecotourism; financial speculation and investment; and expansion of the global seafood and aquaculture sectors. During the past decade, this process has increasingly threatened the survival of small-scale fisheries globally by transforming production methods and resource access (Barbesgaard, 2019; Foley and Mather, 2019; Bennett et al., 2015; TNI, 2014). The Fisheries WG reports:

> As a set of practices regrouping access agreements that harm small-scale fishers, unreported catch, incursions into protected waters, and the diversion of resources away from local populations, *ocean grabbing* is a major threat to our oceans. If unchallenged, it could lead to the significant impoverishment of the fishing reserves and the destructions of ecosystems. Small-scale fisheries communities are particularly affected, as they have to face international agreements systematically diminishing their exclusive fishing areas, compromising their survival and the culture that goes with it. The effects are not limited to the catch itself, as they also affect the complex and rooted post-harvest value chain that develops along the community, and in which women play a crucial role. (IPC, 2019b)

Similarly, coastal grabbing refers to "the appropriation of coastal space — including sea and land — by interests external to the community" (Bavinck et al., 2017, 2). The concept of coastal grabbing emerged in the interest of addressing the connection between land and sea as two spaces that most coastal communities depend on accessing. These grabs are driven by economic interests, such as aquaculture and mining projects, conservation policies like MPAs and political support for rapid economic development. Coastal grabs have two main types of impacts: first, they exclude coastal communities from the spaces and resources they depend on for their livelihoods; and second, they negatively influence communities' motivation and capacity to engage in local conservation activities. The possible socio-ecological damages include lost livelihoods, impoverishment, pollution and environmental degradation, resulting in physical harm, displacement and out-migration (Bavinck et al., 2017).

Fishers' movements have been tracking grabbing processes and the different forms they take and flagging them on international platforms. They have released numerous statements and publications, organized workshops and established the Ocean Grabbing Working Group to strengthen their internal capacity to recognize and respond to it. In one statement, they denounced ocean grabbing and called for social and economic justice, demanding that "serious and implementable action should be taken by the concerned governments against Ocean Grabbing by corporate profiteering interests" (WFFP, 2015b). In another statement, in which the movements rejected an invitation to join the Coastal Fisheries Initiative (CFI)[3] steering committee, they denounced CFI for its top-down approach to coastal fisheries governance and for facilitating ocean grabbing, noting that the lack of inclusion of fishers' organizations and focus on property rights–based fisheries was yet another example of a "privatization process unleashing benefits for a small elite, while dispossessing the majority" (WFFP and WFF, 2015b). WFFP also published a report entitled *Human Rights vs. Property Rights: Implementation and Interpretation of the SSF Guidelines*, which highlights the differences between the two types of rights in fisheries management: "In addition to denouncing the negative effects of property rights-based fisheries programs, small-scale and artisanal fisherfolk have been actively developing and promoting a human rights-based approach to fisheries; this is the backbone of the SSF Guidelines" (WFFP et al., 2016, 9).

In collaboration with two allied research NGOs, TNI and Afrika Kontakt, WFFP co-published a prominent publication, *The Global Ocean Grab: A Primer*, in 2014, sparking an international debate on the topic that soon gained attention from social movements, academics and governments. The primer argues that ocean grabbing is not only about oceans but is "unfolding worldwide across an array of contexts including marine and coastal seawaters, inland waters, rivers and lakes, deltas and wetlands, mangroves and coral reefs" (TNI, 2014, 4). At WFFP's 7th General Assembly in 2017, where WFF and other allied organizations also participated, a workshop on ocean grabbing was held in which movement members from Sri Lanka, Belize, Indonesia and Kenya discussed the ways in which ocean grabbing can take place and gave examples of how it is playing out in local contexts. The workshop resulted in a collaborative list of how ocean grabbing is occurring; who the main actors are behind it; strategies for developing a collective campaign; and a call for fishers' movements to join hands with other movements to protect and uphold the rights of fishers and farmers (WFFP, 2018). Fishers' movements are still discussing how to grapple with and respond to ocean grabbing and related privatization agendas. Considering the complexity of these agendas and the wide array of actors involved, it is often unclear who to direct responses to and what strategies will be the most effective.

Threats Emerging from Industrial Aquaculture Expansion

Aquaculture expansion, a key development of the post-2000 conservation wave in fisheries, is having a huge impact on the future viability of small-scale fisheries and survival of coastal communities. Aquaculture development is a prime example of the privatization policies that punctuate ocean and coastal grabbing, ignoring critical political questions about who should be deciding what species to fish and where and how fishing should occur —

effectively revoking the political agency of fishers themselves (Ertör and Ortega-Cerdà, 2018; TNI, 2014; Nayak and Berkes, 2010). Large-scale industrial aquaculture has rapidly become a dominant "sustainable" solution for addressing the global fisheries crisis and environmental sustainability. Heralded as a win-win solution for both dwindling fish stocks and feeding a growing global population, it has become one of the world's fastest growing food-producing industries. While small-scale food producers have engaged in artisanal aquaculture for centuries, such as in rice paddies in China and in small household ponds in India, industrial aquaculture has been technologically transformed on an unprecedented scale (Gui et al., 2018; FAO, 2018b; TNI, 2014).

The Fisheries WG argues that while aquaculture "can also be found among local communities, it is with the development of the fisheries industrial sector that aquaculture has become an intensive breeding system. If carried out on a large scale and capital-intensive perspective, the result could be the exclusion of the small-scale fisheries from the market" (IPC, 2019b). There has already been a visible impact on the security of small-scale fishers' livelihoods as seafood markets become saturated with aquaculture products and local fishing grounds become polluted by waste from fish pens (Nayak and Berkes, 2010). Moreover, the species favoured for large-scale aquaculture farms are typically those which fetch high prices in markets in the Global North, such as carp, salmon and shrimp, due to increasingly high demand from middle-income consumers (TNI, 2014). This means that most products are destined for international export, with what remains in domestic markets often being too expensive for many to afford or causing fish shortages in local markets that force people to change their eating habits. This has negatively impacted local food systems, particularly in the Global South, and the food security of poor, rural people, increasing their vulnerability (Nayak and Berkes, 2010; Bavinck et al., 2017).

Fishers' movements have been speaking out about large-scale aquaculture development for decades, with many members organizing campaigns and direct actions at the national level. In India in 1992, for example, fishers lobbied and organized huge protests, contributing to a company withdrawing plans to develop a 1,400-hectare industrial shrimp aquaculture project. By 1999, these mobilizations had expanded into an anti-aquaculture protest movement, led by the Fisher Federation, National Fishworkers' Forum (NFF) and WFF, which helped to freeze a controversial aquaculture bill for more than fifteen years (Bavinck et al., 2017; Adduci, 2009). This is an exceptional outcome as in many other cases around the world resistance from social movements has not been able to force the halt of aquaculture development. However, some resistance has effectively managed to delay projects or lead to legal cases in which court rulings call for project terms to be adjusted (Das, 2018; TNI, 2014).

Movement-led actions against aquaculture persist in India and many other countries. Fishers' movements adamantly reject industrial aquaculture in numerous public statements. A notable example is the Bangkok Statement, in which they call upon UN agencies, regional fisheries bodies and national governments to "reverse and prevent the displacement of fishing communities through the privatization of waters and lands of fishing communities for activities that include tourism, aquaculture, defense/military establishments, conservation and industry" and to "reject industrial aquaculture and genetically modified and exotic species in aquaculture" (WFFP, 2008, 1). During WFFP's 5th General Assembly in Pakistan in April 2011, members spoke out against large-scale aquaculture and initiated a global campaign, including national level actions to save natural resources and oppose aquaculture development in Indonesia, Sri Lanka and South Africa, among other countries. One of their press statements noted:

> WFFP wants global governments to introduce sustainable aquaculture instead of promoting commercial interventions, which are destroying natural resources. The firms developing aquaculture in various countries use chemicals in fish feed and catch, destroying natural water resources... All these member organisations represent poor fishers, who are directly involved in fishing and not a single group of rich peoples is with us. When we demand aquaculture reforms, it means saving the freshwater bodies, which are being depleted by commercialisation of aquaculture all over the world. (Fish Site, 2011)

Critical Loss of Aquatic Genetic Resources and Biodiversity

The protection of aquatic genetic resources, or marine genetic resources, involves maintaining genetic diversity among aquatic species and populations. Biodiversity conservation, as it is more commonly known, is an important element of many fisheries governance and management agendas, as an attempt to ensure the sustainable production and trade of seafood from both capture fisheries and aquaculture (FAO, 2020c; Pullin, 2008). Overfishing, overcapacity and the rapid growth of the aquaculture sector have made attention to biodiversity increasingly important, particularly since the 1980s.

Overfishing and overcapacity in fisheries have predominantly emerged from growing numbers of large-scale industrial fishing boats, leading to the rapid depletion of many fish stocks and too many boats chasing too few fish (Greer and Harvey, 2013). FAO reports that between 1974 and 2017, the percentage of global marine fish stocks being overfished at a biologically unsustainable level rose from 10 to 34.2 percent (FAO, 2020c). Meanwhile, large-scale aquaculture based on monoculture production is typically characterized by low genetic diversity. This type of production can cause genetic issues in farmed fish, such as deformities and the rapid spread of diseases. More worrying is that it can lead to genetic contamination among wild species populations that come in contact with farmed fish, either due to proximity, waterborne diseases or because farmed fish escape from their pens (FAO, 2019a; Krøvel et al., 2019). There has been increasing international concern about the widespread loss of biodiversity and degradation of marine and freshwater ecosystems. In addition to overfishing, overcapacity and aquaculture, this stems from pollution, climate change–induced ocean temperature rise and acidification, deep-sea oil drilling and mining, and underwater noise caused by shipping and other human activities (OceanCare, 2020; IPC, 2019b; Greer and Harvey, 2013).

The importance of protecting biodiversity for small-scale fishers and movements is crucial considering their close connection with, and reliance on, delicate coastal and inland aquatic ecosystems. One of the ways that fishers' movements have been engaging with the protection of biodiversity is by participating in the process for upholding the Convention on Biological Diversity (CBD) (IPC, 2019b). Endorsed in 1992 by 150 government leaders at the Rio Earth Summit, CBD is dedicated to promoting sustainable development globally. It is a legally binding instrument for conserving biological diversity, using natural resources sustainably and sharing benefits derived from the use of resources equitably (CBD, 2000). Members of the Fisheries WG told me that they have participated in CBD conferences, meetings, regional workshops, working groups, informal advisory committees; contributed to action plans, frameworks, guidelines and national reporting; and implemented country-level programs and projects.[4] (see also CBD, 2020). The Fisheries WG has released numerous statements, such as on the International Day for Biological Diversity (IDB), asserting the rights of fishing communities to protect biodiversity. On IDB in 2012, which had a marine biodiversity theme, fishers' movements organized country-level events to stress the importance of participatory conservation and management initiatives. They demanded recognition of their rights to access and use resources for their livelihoods, conserve and manage biodiversity and participate in conservation and management processes (CBD, 2012). At the 11th Conference of Parties to the CBD in 2012, WFFP and ICSF made a statement in response to the agenda item Inland Waters Biodiversity:

> With millions of people dependent on inland water fisheries for a livelihood, fishing communities perhaps have one of the largest stakes in ensuring the health of inland waters and their biodiversity. It is important to ensure the participation of Indigenous Peoples and local communities, including fishing communities, in the conservation and sustainable use of inland waters biodiversity if long-term conservation goals are to be met and if the ability of biodiversity to continue to support the water cycle is to be maintained. This would require the integration of the traditional knowledge, practices and rights of the Indigenous Peoples and local communities. Supporting Indigenous Peoples and local communities, particularly fishing communities, to sustainably manage inland waters, by strengthening cooperation on capacity building and governance, promoting secure land and water tenure, and particularly by putting in place participatory decision-making processes and benefit sharing arrangements, is crucial to the conservation of inland water biodiversity and maintenance of the water cycle. (WFFP, 2012)

Detrimental Neglect of Inland Fisheries

Inland capture fisheries carried out in lakes and rivers provide a central source of protein for millions of people, particularly in the African Great Lakes, Lower Mekong Basin, Peruvian and Brazilian Amazon, and Brahmaputra and Ayeyarwady River Basins, where fish consumption per capita is the highest in the world. Several of the largest fish producing countries, such as China, India, Cambodia and Indonesia, have reported an increase in inland production in the last decade, representing 59 percent of inland fish catch globally (FAO, 2020c; Arthur and Friend, 2011). Inland lakes and rivers are severely impacted by environmental and climate fluctuations, such as changes in rainfall and ground water level and drought, as well as human activities, including soil and water salination caused by agricultural run-off, water pollution in urban areas and hydropower development (FAO, 2020c; Funge-Smith and Bennett, 2019; Arthur and Friend, 2011). Despite these critical issues, inland fisheries have received far less international attention from policymakers and researchers than their marine counterparts. The Fisheries WG argues:

> Too often neglected in the international discussions, the internal waters fisheries provide work for more than 60 million people and nutrition for their communities. Most of the internal waters fisheries are located in developing countries, practiced through artisanal methods. Yet, despite the significant importance in certain regions, the effects of land grabbing and the direct and indirect pollution of the waters by extractive and industrial practices, seriously endanger this kind of fishery. (IPC, 2019b)

Despite the important contribution of inland fisheries to both livelihoods and global fish production, inland fishers' catches are underreported. While data collection on marine fisheries has increased steadily in the past few decades, the inland subsector is neglected, leading to a lack of information available on both catches and employment (Funge-Smith and Bennett, 2019; Arthur and Friend, 2011; De Schutter, 2012). FAO reports that millions of tonnes of fish caught by small-scale fishers are invisible, with an estimated 70 percent of the inland fisheries catch underreported. The lack of routine monitoring across diverse inland fisheries makes it extremely difficult to establish a clear picture of the stock levels and health of inland fisheries globally (FAO, 2020c). This lack of attention has not only been an issue in the policymaking and research spheres. Within fishers' movements, there has also been a tendency to focus on oceans and marine fisheries, without providing much space for inland fishers' voices or for addressing the issues affecting them. However, in 2017, WFFP published a ground-breaking report on inland fisheries, which stated:

> Until recently, the voices of millions of inland small-scale fishers, the primary users of freshwater resources and inland streams have been unheard. Indeed, the few studies around inland small-scale fishing, at an international level and at local national levels, have mainly been conducted by the academic and corporate sectors. Initially, the World Forum of Fisher Peoples (WFFP) did not address the state and challenges of small-scale fisheries, even though inland fishing communities represent a significant part of WFFP and its constituency. This started to change in 2015, when a WFFP working group on inland fisheries was created, with the objective to consolidate and strengthen the voice of inland small-scale

> fishers within the organisation and beyond. Central to this was a Human Rights Based approach for the management of inland fisheries and to enhance food sovereignty for inland small-scale fishing communities. (WFFP, 2017, 1)

The report notes that inland fisheries are too often confined to informal or recreational fishing sectors, which overlooks the health, nutritional, cultural and social value of inland fisheries livelihoods. Despite their crucial role in local livelihoods and nutrition, about half of freshwater species globally are not biologically registered in official scientific databases, meaning that they are essentially non-existent in official statistics. This is largely caused by a lack of engagement between researchers and small-scale inland fishing communities and a lack of understanding of artisanal, Indigenous and traditional knowledge. While the definition of inland fisheries used in academic and governmental spheres refers only to harvesting methods, WFFP argues that this definition fails to take fishing communities and livelihoods into account, nor does it speak to food sovereignty practices in fisheries (KNTI and WFFP, 2017).

Fishers' movements have been working toward addressing this gap through the publication of their report, as well as organizing local workshops with inland fishing communities and a knowledge exchange on the state of inland fisheries globally with participants from South Africa, Kenya, Bangladesh and Canada. In WFFP's 7th General Assembly in 2017, participants at an inland fisheries workshop established action points for moving forward and expanding their work. These action points included building alliances around agroecology to rebuild depleted lakes and rivers; learning from experiences in Indonesia and India, where there are strong inland fishers' movements who have participated in policymaking processes; organizing knowledge exchanges between inland fishing communities; strengthening community-based research mechanisms for producing inland fisheries data; resisting dams and industrial projects effecting inland waters; demanding the implementation of the SSF Guidelines in inland waters; and fighting for the recognition of inland fishers' rights to access and govern resources (WFFP, 2018).

Development, Exclusion and Implications for Small-Scale Fishers

The issues at the heart of the movements' struggles are deeply embedded within the overlapping waves of development in fisheries globally, discussed in Chapter 2. These waves, and associated processes of exclusion, have profound impacts on small-scale fisheries, emerging in several ways. First, the expansion of the industrial seafood system has broadened and intensified privatization in fisheries. Second, intensive investment in the "sustainable development" and use of natural resources has extended into new frontiers, namely the oceans. Third, the accelerated spread of mitigation and adaptation initiatives has intersected with conservation agendas, further restricting access to fisheries resources and areas. Fourth, the COVID-19 pandemic has added an additional layer of insecurity for small-scale fishers, exacerbating multiple vulnerabilities in the fisheries sector (Belton et al., 2021; Marschke et al., 2021; Havice et al., 2020). These impacts also illuminate the convergence of four global crises: a (food) production crisis, an investment crisis, an environmental and climate crisis, and a health crisis.

Expansion of the Industrial Seafood System and Privatization

The expansion of the industrial seafood system has broadened and intensified privatization in fisheries, concentrating property, wealth and power in the hands of large-scale industrial fishing companies. Privatization agendas are illustrative of a type of wealth-based fisheries management being promoted by international financial agencies like the World Bank, an approach which aims to limit the leakage of resource rent from the sector (Biswas, 2011; Høst, 2015). Controversy over how to deal with "property and rent have long been at the heart of debates over the growing fisheries crisis, a debate that is gaining attention because of the importance of fisheries in ecological systems, food security and economic development" (Campling and Havice, 2014, 723). Fishing areas are not only key sites of production contributing to the global food system, but they are also crucial for the livelihoods of small-scale fishers and coastal communities (Jentoft, 2019; Barbesgaard, 2018). Yet, the push for privatization in fisheries has been led by state and private sector interests in harmonizing social and environmental norms with economic efficiency. In other words, packaging everything up into tidy private property and access rights is presented as a way to make the sector simultaneously more manageable, sustainable and profitable (Biswas, 2011; Pinkerton, 2017).

One prominent example of the privatization process has been the implementation of fishing quota systems, such as individual transferable quotas (ITQs) to control access to fisheries resources (Longo et al., 2015; Sundar, 2012). As mentioned in Chapter 2, ITQs are used by many governments around the world to regulate fishing and adhere to limits established by sustainability measurements (Bromley, 2016). These systems facilitate the emergence of competitive quota markets, in which large industrial fishing companies obtain several quotas from other fishers, further entrenching private ownership and access to and control over fisheries resources. In many prominent ITQ-implementing countries, such as Iceland, Canada, Namibia, South Africa, New Zealand and Chile, the allocation of fishing quotas has excluded many fishers from the sector by restricting commercial fisheries to a few core fishers and fishing companies (Arnason, 2002; Bodwitch, 2017; Ibarra et al., 2000; Pinkerton, 2017). Fishers often end up selling their quotas because this brings in more money than they would get from fishing; they are unable to sell their entire catch on the market because of industrial competition; or dwindling fish stocks prevent them from catching enough to make a living. Quota systems exacerbate the concentration of wealth and power in the industrial fisheries sector, while intensifying inequality, poverty and livelihood insecurity in small-scale fishing communities (Jentoft, 2019; Jones et al., 2017; Longo et al., 2015; Sundar, 2012; Isaacs, 2011; Isaacs and Hara, 2015).

Intensification of Investment in "Sustainable Development"

The second impact is that intensive investment in the "sustainable development" of natural resources has extended beyond forests and agricultural lands and into new territories and frontiers — particularly the oceans and inland fishing areas. The sustainable development approach promises to provide economic growth and opportunities while simultaneously protecting the environment and ensuring resources will continue to be productive. This approach has become especially prominent in the context of the UN's Sustainable Development Goals (SDGs), which aim to link economic, social and environmental development. The focus on sustainability also brings the UN's environment agenda to the fore and prioritizes the development of sustainable consumption and production patterns globally (Gasper et al., 2019; UN, 2015a). This discourse has been criticized as one "devoted to the rational management of scarce resources so that nature can continue to serve as a material base for capital accumulation well into the twenty-first century" (Steinberg, 1999, 403). In recent years, both freshwater and marine areas have increasingly become the target of sustainable development agendas — especially due to the rise in land conflicts spurred by development projects that cut off local communities' access to forests and agricultural land. Investors often approach oceans as if they are a lawless frontier full of natural resources up for grabs (Campling and Colás, 2021;

Ertör and Ortega-Cerdà, 2018) or a "frontier replete with opportunity, at last capable of being 'conquered'" (Steinberg, 1999, 404).

A prominent example of this intensification is investment being poured into the development of aquaculture, as a "sustainable" solution for addressing dwindling fisheries resources. Aquaculture expansion, which has been called the fisheries sector's newest commodity frontier (Saguin, 2016), is presented as a way to address growing global demand, address overfishing by decreasing pressure on wild fish stocks and support sustainability and the conservation of aquatic ecosystems by limiting fishing activity. It has quickly become one of the world's fastest growing food-producing industries, with aquaculture sectors expanding around the world, from Chile to Norway and Turkey to China (see Ertör and Ortega-Cerdà, 2018; Gui et al., 2018; Krøvel et al., 2019). This rapid increase is having a significant effect on small-scale fishers' ability to maintain their livelihoods, due to intensified market competition and ecological impact. The speed and scale at which aquaculture can produce allows huge quantities of fish to be sold for relatively low prices, effectively saturating the market and making it difficult for small-scale fishers to compete (Rigby et al., 2017). Many industrial fishing companies have also increasingly targeted small fish, such as anchovies, to sell to fishmeal factories to process into feed for aquaculture fish — exhausting stocks which many small-scale fishers are highly dependent on (Ertör and Ortega-Cerdà, 2018). Aquatic ecosystems are further impacted by fish-pen waste collecting on the sea floor, water contamination caused by worn down facilities and production inputs like growth hormones and antibiotics, and the spread of diseases. These issues impact the present and future viability of wild fish stocks and the health of the ecosystems that small-scale fishers' livelihoods depend on (Gui et al., 2018; Krøvel et al., 2019).

Accelerating Spread of Climate Change Initiatives

The third impact is that the accelerated spread of climate change mitigation and adaptation initiatives, and their intersection with conservation agendas, further restricts access to fisheries resources and areas. This acceleration is perhaps most prominent in the context of land-based initiatives like REDD+ (reducing emissions from deforestation and forest degradation), involving the sale of carbon credits as a way to prevent deforestation, offset existing and future emissions and slow global warming (Scheidel, 2019; Beymer-Farris and Bassett, 2012), but more recently has seeped into fisheries. Fishing areas where climate change mitigation and adaptation overlap with food production policies are central points for the emergence of the global "climate-food system." In this system, "new" initiatives, such as climate-smart agriculture, forestry and fisheries (CSA) and blue growth, are presented as win-win solutions to address destructive production practices, environmental degradation and climate change–induced natural disasters. However, despite promising benefits for all, many small-scale producers end up losing either partial or complete access to resources and are excluded from potential benefits (Clapp et al., 2018; Barbesgaard, 2018; Hunsberger et al., 2017; Martinez-Alier et al., 2016).

A key part of this accelerated spread is that in global and national climate governance agendas, development initiatives are increasingly being reframed as mitigation and adaptation efforts. Such agendas have begun to prioritize adaptation measures over mitigation efforts as the effects of climate change — particularly coastal storms and sea level rise — become more frequent and severe sooner than predicted. Some governments have turned to the private sector to act as development sponsors and manage adaptation initiatives, shifting the social and economic responsibility away from the state. In some cases, coastal development projects have been presented as part of a national adaptation strategy — such as relocating fishing communities for their protection only to subsequently use vacated areas for high-end tourist resorts and other development projects (Uson, 2017; Segi, 2014). Such projects prioritize private interests over the protection of fishers' livelihoods and the environments they depend on while facilitating the expansion of capitalist development in coastal areas and creating more opportunities for private companies, in partnership with governments, to accumulate capital under the guise of climate change adaptation efforts (Longo et al., 2015). This is just one example of the complex politics that exist within climate governance agendas, in which economic and technological fixes are offered up to address environmental limits and resource overexploitation instead of addressing the core causes of degradation (Dressler et al., 2014; Arsel and Büscher, 2012)

Impacts of the COVID-19 Pandemic

The fourth impact, stemming from the COVID-19 pandemic, has emerged much more recently than the previous three. The pandemic has both illuminated and exacerbated multiple vulnerabilities in the fisheries sector, including dependence on international trade and markets; the insecurity of fisheries livelihoods; and the lack of access to healthcare and other social services in fishing communities (Belton et al., 2021; Marschke et al., 2021; Havice et al., 2020). People in every corner of the world have been affected, with impacts in poor, rural and Indigenous communities, where healthcare services are often unreliable and inaccessible, being especially disproportionate and severe (IPC, 2021a; ICSF, 2020). Fishers and fishing communities have been hit hard on a number of fronts, including health impacts and deaths, loss of livelihoods and new obstacles to accessing seafood markets. In countless countries, fisheries were closed because fishing boats and processing facilities could not provide enough space for people to safely work together (FAO, 2020d; Guttal, 2020; Bennett et al., 2020). The closure of restaurants, hotels and other tourism facilities, particularly in the first months of the pandemic, caused a drastic drop in demand for seafood. This meant a huge loss of income for many fishers, particularly those without access to processing, storage or freezing facilities, who are dependent on selling fresh fish daily. Many became solely reliant on selling their catches in small local markets or directly to consumers. However, such sales typically account for a small fraction of what many fishers and fish sellers need to sell to secure an adequate and stable income (Belton et al., 2021; Bennett et al., 2020; Marschke et al., 2021; Havice et al., 2020; Guttal, 2020; FAO, 2020d).

The impacts of the COVID-19 pandemic have illuminated significant vulnerabilities in the seafood sector, such as the dependence on domestic and international trade. The high perishability of seafood makes it difficult to transport without first processing it, either by freezing, canning or packaging, salting or smoking it. In many places, huge amounts of seafood had to be thrown back into the sea because they could not be sold in time (Havice et al., 2020; Jamwal, 2020; Ananth, 2020). Fishers in many countries begged their governments to direct pandemic support funds toward fisheries or provide them with some form of debt relief to allow them to survive until they were able to work again (Guttal, 2020; Jordan, 2020; Prendergast, 2020). The COVID-19 pandemic represents an unprecedented and historic global moment across all sectors, and fisheries have certainly felt the full force of it. While the short-term impacts of the pandemic are already visible, bigger questions remain of what the longer-term impacts in the global seafood system will be, particularly for the already-vulnerable small-scale sector. However, while this global crisis has created critical obstacles and setbacks in global struggles against poverty and food insecurity, it has also reminded us of the importance of the indivisible linkages between human rights, food, health, and environmental systems. It has shed new light on the crucial and ongoing work that is being done to integrate the universal right to food and the rights of fishers and fishing communities to secure lives and livelihoods, offering an opportunity to build forward better (ICSF, 2020; Clapp and Moseley, 2020; HLPE, 2020).

Concluding Remarks

The fisheries sector is rife with contentious issues and politics, which have only become more complex in recent decades because of global food and climate crises. The IPC Fisheries WG has played a crucial role in framing and voicing the perspectives of small-scale fishers' organizations on international platforms like FAO and raising the profile of the threats and issues small-scale fishers are facing globally. Their prioritization of the blue economy and growth, ocean and coastal grabbing, aquaculture, aquatic genetic resources and biodiversity and inland fisheries have demonstrated their capacities to track and analyze global debates related to fisheries and the oceans and to connect these debates with developments on the ground and material impacts in fishing communities. This provides a critical link between abstract global governance processes and the tangible issues and obstacles that small-scale fishers are experiencing — illustrating one of the most fundamental contributions transnational fishers' movements make to the politics of fisheries. Illuminating these connections also allows us to see how fishers are impacted by the material consequences of the three waves of uneven capitalist development in global fisheries and the expansion of capital, privatization and corporate interests, which have transformed the sector and contributed to both regional and intersectoral disparities (Fraser, 2021; Olin Wright, 2019; O'Connor, 1998).

Fishers' movements recognize the flaws in global systems of production, circulation and consumption and are resisting the exclusionary concentration of power and control this system fosters. They also recognize that effective resistance is not only about challenging the dominant system but about developing and voicing alternative strategies and solutions for building a system based on social justice, human rights and equity. In advocating for these alternatives, fishers' movements play an important role in international spaces and platforms. However, systemic constraints and small-scale fishers' marginalization have also meant that fishers' movements have not always been able to respond and mobilize as they wish. They have had to be both creative and cautious in their engagement with contentious issues, figuring out when and how to address particular issues, in which spaces and in collaboration with which strategic allies. They have also had to be pragmatic about their human, time and financial capacities — targeting particular issues, while neglecting others depending on what is feasible at a given moment. Some issues, such as labour and trade policy, may be seen from both outside and inside the movements as silences which they should consider giving more attention to in internal capacity-building and advocacy work. Yet, despite the ever-evolving politics of global fisheries and the steady flow of challenges fishers' movements have made notable progress in expanding their knowledge and analyses and contributing their perspectives to public forums.

NOTES

1. FIAN International is a global human rights organization that advocates for the right to adequate food and nutrition.
2. TBTI was established in 2013 as a research network of social scientists from universities around the world working on small-scale fisheries issues.
3. Coastal Fisheries Initiative (CFI) is a global effort funded by the Global Environment Facility, which brings together United Nations agencies and international conservation organizations, aiming to improve fisheries management and conserve marine biodiversity in coastal areas through better governance and strengthening the seafood value chain (FAO, 2020a).
4. One notable example is the *Time for a Sea Change* study on Thailand published by ICSF (see Prasertcharoensuk and Shott, 2010).

6 Capacities, Alliances, Critical Voices and the Future of Fisheries Justice

In exploring why and how transnational fishers' movements contest and seek to influence the politics of global fisheries, this book illuminates four key arguments. First, overlapping processes of exclusion stemming from decades of industrialization and privatization in fisheries globally and more recent intersections with conservation agendas have both triggered and are propelling transnational mobilization as fishers seek ways to respond to exclusion, dispossession and exploitation. Second, fishers' movements' engagement with fisheries, food and climate politics and related international political processes, have been crucial catalysts in both internal capacity-building and forming productive alliances with other civil society and intergovernmental organizations. Third, fishers' movements contribute an essential critical voice to international political spaces focused on fisheries, food and climate governance by analyzing and challenging agendas and initiatives put forward by governments and intergovernmental bodies and providing feedback on how they can become more viable and just. Fourth, fishers' movements play a key role in raising the profile of the threats and issues small-scale fishers are facing globally by continuously flagging these in international platforms and through their advocacy campaigns and statements. These key points are elaborated upon below, followed by a discussion on critical issues for fisheries, food and climate governance and challenges and ways forward for fisheries justice activism.

Overlapping Processes of Exclusion Propelling Mobilization

Historical and structural developments in global fisheries reveal three distinct overlapping waves: the industrialization wave (post-1900); the privatization wave (post-1970); and the conservation wave (post-2000). These three waves have in turn facilitated overlapping processes of exclusion in the fisheries sector, involving dispossession of small-scale fishers from accessing fishing areas and resources; insecure livelihoods; and conflicts caused by dwindling fish stocks and intensified competition for resources (Longo et al., 2015). The consequences of such processes have facilitated significant transformations in global fisheries, involving shifting socio-economic relations between fishers, markets and consumers. Many small-scale fishers have lost access to markets, been dispossessed from their means of production and had their labour exploited by owners of industrial fishing companies. Governance mechanisms have focused too narrowly on the management and conservation of fisheries resources while failing to address deeper structural inequalities and concentration of power in the sector. This system has also cast fishers as subjects of development, which themselves need to be managed and controlled, rather than providing space in which they can contribute to fisheries governance and resource conservation (Campling et al., 2012).

Yet, fishing communities are also transforming as they seek ways to adapt to socio-economic shifts, develop creative ways to continue to survive in the sector and demonstrate their capacities to be agents of change. The emergence of WFFP and WFF has been a vivid illustration of the creativity and political capacities within these communities, which have found ways to organize locally and nationally and subsequently scale up their struggles to the transnational level. The complexity of the fisheries sector has required the movements to develop diverse resistance strategies and tools for mobilization — including producing statements, research and reports; organizing assemblies, meetings and workshops; building alliances with like-minded and supportive organizations; engaging directly in intergovernmental and civil society spaces; and in some cases, choosing principled non-participation. These strategies and tools have been employed with varying degrees of consistency since the 1990s, which has been reflected in the movements' level of activity, visibility and cohesion. None of these elements have been historically static but have ebbed and flowed as a result of shifting global political and economic contexts and internal capacities (Tarrow, 2011). Fishers' movements have mobilized around and contributed to debates and processes within broader civil society and fisheries governance arenas to explicitly challenge mainstream visions and norms that neglect fishers' human rights and fail to protect the future viability of the small-scale sector. In the context of increasingly complex politics around seafood production, circulation and consumption, the role of fishers' movements as actors that are challenging the current state of affairs and raising critical perspectives becomes all the more crucial.

Internal Capacity-Building and Forming Productive Alliances

Maintaining cohesion within transnational movements like WFFP and WFF is a continuous challenge, particularly due to the diverse national contexts of members and infrequent direct contact between them. The heterogeneity of members can cause internal tensions and conflict, which sometimes can be addressed and smoothed over, while at other times these tensions boil over and create fractures. In the fishers' movements, this became particularly evident leading up to and during the 2000 split in Loctudy. The split was the consequence of a combination of tensions around both the political direction and purpose of WFF and leadership dynamics in which the strong and at times inflexible characters of particular individuals were a determining factor in the decisive outcome. This effectively divided the international network of individuals and organizations fighting for the rights of small-scale fishers. This pivotal moment likely had a long-term impact on the mobilizing strength of both WFF and WFFP by spreading advocacy around small-scale fisheries thinly across two movements rather than concentrating the work in one unified base.

On the other hand, the split may have opened new mobilization paths in which both movements could develop and pursue political agendas that better suited their respective memberships. Having the members divided into two allied camps may have prevented future stalemates emerging in discussions around agenda-setting, strategy and actions to organize. In the following years, while maintaining similar constitutional bases and focusing on drawing attention to similar structural issues in small-scale fisheries, WFF and WFFP evolved into different movements with different political characters. Yet the SSF Guidelines development process provided a crucial opportunity for the two movements, in collaboration with ICSF and FAO, to re-build and strengthen their alliance with each other. The success of this process required a great deal of energy and mobilization, especially from particular committed individuals within the four organizations, without which the Guidelines may have taken a very different form or may have never come to fruition. The role of fishers' movements in the Guidelines process is one prominent example of how they have developed their capacities to critically analyze global structural inequality and unequal power relations; effectively negotiated intergovernmental spaces; and centred their advocacy work on a human rights–based approach to addressing small-scale fishers' social, political and economic marginalization (Ratner et al., 2014). The movements' ability to recognize the power of human rights principles and the importance of developing international guidelines for small-scale fisheries, and to access and actively participate in this process, emerged from a series of historical events and developments. In combination, the UN's post-1990s opening up to civil society engagement; the rise of social movement opposition to private property agendas; and their recognition of the essentiality of human and tenure rights in their struggles highlight how historical events are continuously influencing each other and creating new possibilities for the future (McKeon, 2017a; Ratner et al., 2014).

Contributing a Critical Voice to International Political Spaces

The UN's COFI, CFS and COP are three international political spaces that have been significant for global fisheries, food and climate governance. They have also involved active, long-term engagement from fishers' movements and contributed to shaping some aspects of their political agendas and the issues they prioritize. Fishers' movements have participated in these spaces in different ways, which provides important insights into the diverse forms of social movement engagement that emerge at the transnational level. They have participated more directly in COFI and CFS through their membership in the IPC and CSM, while they have engaged more indirectly with COP through their participation in parallel civil society–led climate justice spaces. the IPC, CSM and parallel COP-related events have also been crucial convergence and alliance-building spaces, which have played a key role in capacity-building within fishers' movements.

The political spaces mapped in this book provide important insights into how moments and events that have taken place in the past have made important contributions to shaping fishers' movements current political strategies and character. At the same time, the movements have made important contributions to these international spaces and events by voicing the concerns of small-scale fishers and advocating for the protection of their rights, lives and livelihoods. They have raised critical questions, challenged mainstream governance agendas and offered constructive ways for fishers' knowledge and experience to be taken more centrally into account. However, as mobilization and active participation have ebbed and flowed over time, the movements have faced internal capacity issues, in terms of human and financial resources and analytical capabilities, which have posed obstacles to their participation in other relevant international spaces addressing fisheries and related issues. They continue to struggle to assert their right to a seat at the table in intergovernmental UN spaces and will need to keep strengthening their political skills and expanding their mobilization efforts in order to maintain their role in these spaces.

Raising the Profile of Small-Scale Fisheries Issues

Contentious politics and issues are core factors shaping the character of global fisheries and fishers' movements and determining why and how movements raise their voices, contest and resist. Several key issues have shaped fishers' movements' anti-capitalist struggles, becoming focal points of their political agendas and central threads connecting them to particular international debates, spaces and platforms. Through their participation in the IPC Fisheries Working Group, fishers' movements have narrowed in on the blue economy and growth, ocean and coastal grabbing, aquaculture, aquatic genetic resources and biodiversity, and inland fisheries. By analyzing and engaging with these issues in statements, reports, briefs, workshops, webinars and FAO spaces and events, the Fisheries WG has played a crucial role in guiding movement engagement with COFI and CFS, while also contributing to shaping movement discourse in international intergovernmental, civil society and research spaces. Fishers' movements have an important role to play in analyzing capitalist development and the consequences of neoliberal globalization and connecting these broad processes with particular local contexts and fishers' experiences. This ability to create connections between abstract global debates and related governance processes and tangible issues faced by small-scale fishers is a vital contribution transnational movements make to both fisheries politics and to strengthening fisheries justice efforts.

Such connections provide important insights into how small-scale fishers are being unjustly impacted by capitalist development in the fisheries sector and how the expansion of capital, corporate interests and privatization have transformed the sector. Such expansions have contributed to regional and intersectoral inequalities and had profound social and economic consequences for fishers. Yet, despite systemic constraints and marginalization, fishers' movements have made valuable contributions to raising the profile of small-scale fisheries issues at the global level, finding creative ways to voice critical concerns through a combination of written documents, public actions and strategic collaboration with civil society and academic and intergovernmental actors. At times, they have been criticized by governments and intergovernmental organizations for being too radical in their demands or being difficult to collaborate with because they have refused to compromise on issues that that they believed were non-negotiable. Their alliances and organizational relationships have shifted over time as interests and objectives have changed. Some of these alliances and relationships have been strengthened, while others have been weakened or dissolved altogether. Yet, despite the constantly changing global context and the continuous flux of challenges being presented to small-scale fishers, fishers' movements have continued to inform themselves about emerging issues, expand their agendas and find ways to make themselves heard.

Critical Issues for Fisheries, Food and Climate Governance

Moving toward the future, if small-scale fishers are to be appropriately and effectively supported by their governments, there are several critical issues that must be addressed in fisheries, food and climate governance. Small-scale fishers, their organizations and movements should be provided space to directly participate in policymaking processes that directly affect their lives and livelihoods. This participation should be organized in different forms locally, nationally and internationally in order to ensure their knowledge and perspectives are being taken into account in different contexts and by governments at all levels. As an international instrument developed by small-scale fishers' organizations, the *Voluntary Guidelines for Securing Sustainable Small-Scale Fisheries in the Context of Food Security and Poverty Eradication* (SSF Guidelines) should be implemented more widely by all the COFI members that endorsed them in 2014. This implementation, and the subsequent monitoring of implementation, should be done in close collaboration with national fishers' organizations which work directly with local fishing communities. Furthermore, initiatives being scaled up as part of blue economy and blue growth agendas, such as marine protected areas (MPAS), coastal development, blue carbon credit systems, off-shore energy and aquaculture expansion, should not be implemented without effective consultation with fishing and coastal communities. This includes providing adequate information about proposed initiatives to communities so they are able participate effectively in discussions and consultations. Considering the increasingly complex nature of the fisheries sector, particularly at the global level, governments should make more concerted efforts to collect information and analyses that strengthen their understanding of the challenges fishers face. This means more resources should be devoted to research, particularly qualitative social research, which can contribute toward the development of more effective and equitable governance approaches.

In relation to food policy (including production, circulation and consumption), it is critical that this field engage more directly with fisheries, particularly the small-scale sector, as an essential contributor to global food security and nutrition. Rather than addressing it as a sub-sector of agriculture, fisheries should be recognized as a separate sector with a central role in providing food to the global population, with fishers being given more attention in policy focusing on support for small-scale producers. Policy related to climate change mitigation and adaptation efforts should also engage more directly with how fisheries, fishers and fishing communities are impacted by initiatives intended to address climate impacts and protect coastal areas. This includes direct consultation with fishers and fishers' organizations during the development phase of initiatives that will impact the areas where they live and work and conducting more research on the potential social and cultural consequences of such initiatives. Furthermore, fisheries, food and climate policy should be developed and implemented in a more integrated and holistic manner, rather than using a siloed approach to address issues. This means that decision-making processes and spaces should be more closely linked and those making the decisions should engage more directly and share knowledge and insights at local, national and international levels. Intergovernmental UN processes in particular, such as COFI, CFS and COP, which address intersecting global issues, should be better integrated in order to ensure the development of more effective and comprehensive governance instruments.

Challenges and Ways Forward for Fisheries Justice Activism

Beyond academic and policy debates, there are several key challenges which need to be undertaken in efforts to enhance and expand fisheries justice activism. Strengthening internal capacity within WFFP and WFF is essential, including increasing regular communication and interactions between members; developing more political training programs to ensure analytical and leadership skills are more widely dispersed across the membership; building the capacities of leaders to enable them to be more active and engaged in agenda-setting and activities; and expanding membership into more countries. Maintaining momentum, particularly during ebbs in energy and mobilization, is also important to ensuring the progress made in movement-building during more vibrant, active moments is preserved. This can be done, for example, by focusing on internal capacity-building during quieter moments, such as in between general assemblies, biennial COFI sessions and other important international events. Finding ways to balance national and international work is an important part of this, in order to ensure that national struggles are not neglected due to limited human capacity being directed toward international agendas. This involves providing more information on the purpose and significance of international work to local and national organizations and actors within the movements to illustrate the value of international participation.

Strengthening alliances and collaboration between WFFP and WFF, and with civil society groups, researchers and intergovernmental organizations, as well as building new alliances with potential allies, is essential for creating wider networks for sharing strategies and developing collective actions, learning from each other and scaling up national and transnational advocacy. Alliances and collaborations can be bolstered by connecting small-scale fisheries issues and debates with those related to food production, circulation and consumption and climate change impacts and mitigation. These connections are vital for making small-scale fisheries issues more widely visible and taken into account by a larger number of actors in governance and policymaking spheres. Increasing this visibility should involve more efforts, through public actions, statements, research and reports, to insert fisheries issues into food and climate discussions, which have typically been more focused on agriculture and land. Finally, retaining a seat at the table in international spaces such as COFI and CFS is crucial to ensuring that fishers' movements continue to play a role in fisheries and food discussions, and related politics, and that the interests and perspectives of small-scale fishers are fairly and adequately represented in these spaces. This involves more active participation in respected movement-led platforms, such as the IPC and CSM, and preparing a wider range of members to effectively engage in and contribute insights and messages to these platforms.

The struggles of small-scale fishers are far from over and in many ways are only becoming more challenging in an era of rising political support and investment in blue agendas. Social movements more broadly are losing traction in some international processes and spaces, as the interests of more powerful political and economic actors squeeze them out or co-opt their agendas. Yet this may also encourage movements to locate other relevant spaces that are worthwhile to devote energy to beyond those they have traditionally prioritized and participated in. Alliances and collaborations between movements and scholar-activists are more important than ever for sharpening political analysis, sharing resources, developing more powerful strategies and strengthening and expanding social justice efforts. As this book shows, even in the face of complex international challenges, social movements continue to have hope, resist unjust and unsustainable agendas and find creative ways to critically engage in politics. The struggle continues.

Acknowledgements

My heartfelt gratitude to the members of the World Forum of Fisher Peoples (WFFP), the World Forum of Fish Harvesters and Fish Workers (WFF) and interviewees from numerous allied organizations for your openness, conversations, knowledge, insights and archival information, which have provided crucial inspiration and material for this research. Your invaluable contributions have made this research possible. Thank you to the Masifundise staff in Cape Town for graciously providing access to their incredible fishers' movements archive and for being such welcoming hosts. Special thanks to Andy Johnston for building that archive, for warmly welcoming me into your home and for generously sharing your personal collection of videos and photos — many of which can be found in this book. You have played a crucial role in preserving the rich history of the fishers' movements.

Thank you to the inspiring and supportive International Institute of Social Studies (ISS) community, and particularly the "villagers," who made the PhD journey a lot less lonely and a lot more fun. Moving to The Hague ten years ago, I never could have imagined what an amazing group of friends and colleagues I would end up with all around the world. Many thanks to Des Gasper, Jessica Duncan, Oane Visser, Martha Robbins, Maarten Bavinck, Charles Levkoe, Moenieba Isaacs, Tony Charles and Murat Arsel for your feedback and encouragement at various stages of the research process. Special thanks to my PhD supervisor, Jun Borras, for being such an inspiring mentor and supporter, the opportunities you have given me, the intellectual doors you have opened, your enthusiasm and good humour, the "village" dinners in your garden and for encouraging me to push myself further than I thought possible. I am so grateful for everything.

I would also like to thank the entire Fernwood team and the editors of the *Critical Development Studies* series for the opportunity to publish this book as part of their inspiring collection and for their excellent editorial work and guidance every step of the way.

To my International Collective in Support of Fishworkers (ICSF) colleagues, thank you for welcoming me so warmly into the community and for all the inspiring conversations and collaborations. I look forward to many more. To friends and colleagues at the Transnational Institute (TNI), thank you for countless discussions on the many overlapping layers of fisheries and movement politics and for introducing me to members of WFFP and WFF in Paris in 2015.

Thank you to my friends near and far for all of your love, encouragement and emotional support. To my Canadian and Dutch families, thank you for believing in me and encouraging me to keep going despite some very difficult times. I am so lucky to have all of you. Thanks to my late father for his wisdom and for teaching me the art of debate and appreciation for late night discussions about the state of the world. Special thanks to my mum, the strongest and most hardworking woman I know; you taught me never to give up on the things that are important to me, no matter how challenging they may be. And finally, thank you to Emiel, for being such an incredible partner, friend and my biggest fan. Thank you for everything.

References

Adduci, M. (2009). Neoliberal wave rocks Chilika Lake, India: Conflict over intensive aquaculture from a class perspective. *Journal of Agrarian Change*, 9(4), 484–511.

Ahmadun, F.R., Wong, M.M.R., and Said, A.M. (2020). Consequences of the 2004 Indian ocean tsunami in Malaysia. *Safety Science*, 121, 619–631.

Allison, E.H. (2001). Big laws, small catches: Global ocean governance and the fisheries crisis. *Journal of International Development*, 13(7), 933–950.

Ananth, M.K. (2020). COVID-19 lockdown: Fish in stock, but fishermen at sea. *India Times*, April 1. <https://timesofindia.indiatimes.com/india/ covid-19-lockdown-fish-in-stock-but-fishermen-at-sea/articleshow/74915587.cms>.

Andrée, P., Clark, J.K., Levkoe, C.Z., and Lowitt, K. (2019). Introduction–Traversing theory and practice: Social movement engagement in food systems governance for sustainability, justice, and democracy. In *Civil Society and Social Movements in Food System Governance*, 1–18. Routledge.

Arnason, R. (2005). Property rights in fisheries: Iceland's experience with ITQs. *Reviews in Fish Biology and Fisheries*, 15(3), 243–264.

____. (2002). *A Review of International Experiences with ITQs*. Portsmouth: Centre for the Economics and Management of Aquatic Resources.

Arsel, M., and Büscher, B. (2012). Nature™ Inc.: Changes and continuities in neoliberal conservation and market-based environmental policy. *Development and Change*, 43(1), 53–78.

Arthur, R.I., and Friend, R.M. (2011). Inland capture fisheries in the Mekong and their place and potential within food-led regional development. *Global Environmental Change*, 21(1), 219–226.

Barbesgaard, M. (2019). Ocean and land control-grabbing: The political economy of landscape transformation in Northern Tanintharyi, Myanmar. *Journal of Rural Studies*, 69, 195–203.

____. (2018). Blue growth: Savior or ocean grabbing? *The Journal of Peasant Studies*, 45(1), 130–149.

Bauböck, R. (2003). Towards a political theory of migrant transnationalism. *International Migration Review*, 37(3), 700–723.

Bavinck, M., Berkes, F., Charles, A., et al. (2017). The impact of coastal grabbing on community conservation—A global reconnaissance. *Maritime Studies*, 16(1), 8.

Belton, B., Rosen, L., Middleton, L., et al. (2021). COVID-19 impacts and adaptations in Asia and Africa's aquatic food value chains. *Marine Policy*, 129, 104523.

Béné, C. (2003). When fishery rhymes with poverty: A first step beyond the old paradigm on poverty in small-scale fisheries. *World Development*, 31(6), 949–975.

Bennett, N.J., Blythe, J., White, C.S., and Campero, C. (2021). Blue growth and blue justice: Ten risks and solutions for the ocean economy. *Marine Policy*, 125.

Bennett, N.J., Cisneros-Montemayor, A.M., Blythe, J., et al. (2019). Towards a sustainable and equitable blue economy. *Nature Sustainability*, 2(11), 991–993.

Bennett, N.J., Finkbeiner, E.M., Ban, N.C., et al. (2020). The COVID-19 pandemic, small-scale fisheries and coastal fishing communities. *Coastal Management*, 48(4), 336–347.

Bennett, N., Govan, H. and Satterfield, T. (2015). Ocean grabbing. *Marine Policy*, 57, 61–68.

Beymer-Farris, B., and Bassett, T. (2012). The REDD menace: Resurgent protectionism in Tanzania's mangrove forests. *Global Environmental Change*, 22, 332–341.

Biswas, N. (2011). Turning the tide: Women's lives in fisheries and the assault of capital. *Economic and Political Weekly*, 46(51), 53–60.

Bodwitch, H. (2017). Challenges for New Zealand's individual transferable quota system: Processor consolidation, fisher exclusion, & Māori quota rights. *Marine Policy*, 80(October 2016), 88–95.

Borras, S.M. (2016). Land politics, agrarian movements and scholar-activism. Inaugural lecture, International Institute of Social Studies, 14 April.

Borras, S.M., and Franco, J.C. (2012). Global land grabbing and trajectories of agrarian change: A preliminary analysis. *Journal of Agrarian Change*, 12(1), 34–59.

Borras, S.M., Moreda, T., Alonso-Fradejas, A., and Brent, Z.W. (2018). Converging social justice issues and movements: Implications for political actions and research. *Third World Quarterly*, 39(7), 1227–1246.

Brem-Wilson, J. (2015). Towards food sovereignty: Interrogating peasant voice in the United Nations Committee on World Food Security. *The Journal of Peasant Studies*, 42(1), 73–95.

Bromley, D. (2016). Rights-based fisheries and contested claims of ownership: Some necessary clarifications. *Marine Policy*, 72, 231–236.

____. (2009). Abdicating Responsibility: The Deceits of Fisheries Policy. *Fisheries*, 34(6), 280–290.

Bulkeley, H., and Newell, P. (2010). *Governing Climate Change*. Global Institutions Series. Routledge.

Butcher, J.G. (2004). The closing of the frontier: A history of the marine fisheries of Southeast Asia, c. 1850–2000 (No. 8). Institute of Southeast Asian Studies.

Campling, L., and Colás, A. (2021). *Capitalism and the Sea: The Maritime Factor in the Making of the Modern World*. London: Verso Books.

Campling, L., and Havice, E. (2014). The problem of property in industrial fisheries. *The Journal of Peasant Studies*, 41(5), 707–727.

Campling, L., Havice, E., and McCall Howard, P. (2012). The political economy and ecology of capture fisheries: market dynamics, resource access and relations of exploitation and resistance. *Journal of Agrarian Change*, 12(2–3), 177–203.

Castle, S. (2017). As wild salmon decline, Norway pressures its fish farms. *The Seattle Times*, November 7. <https://www.seattletimes.com/nation-world/as-wild-salmon-decline-norway-pressures-its-fish-farms/>.

CBD (Convention on Biological Diversity). (2020). Official website. <https://www.cbd.int/>.

___. (2012). *Fishing Communities Celebrate International Day of Biodiversity (IDB)*. <https://sites.google.com/site/idbfishworkers/home>.

___. (2000). *Sustaining Life on Earth: How the Convention on Biological Diversity Promites Nature and Human Well-Being*. <https://www.cbd.int/doc/publications/cbd-sustain-en.pdf>.

CFS (Committee on World Food Security). (2021). *CFS Voluntary Guidelines on Food Systems and Nutrition*. Rome. <https://www.fao.org/cfs/vgfsn/en/>.

___. (2014). *Policy Recommendations: Sustainable Fisheries and Aquaculture for Food Security and Nutrition*. <http://www.fao.org/3/av032e/ av032e.pdf>.

___. (2010). *Proposal for an International Food Security and Nutrition Civil Society Mechanism for Relations with CFS*. Rome. <http://www.csm4cfs.org/wp-content/uploads/2016/03/Proposal-for-an-international-civil-society-mechanism.pdf>.

Charles, A. (2011). Small-scale fisheries: On rights, trade and subsidies. *MAST*, 10(2), 85–94.

Charles, A., Garcia, S.M., and Rice, J. (2014). A tale of two streams: Synthesizing governance of marine fisheries and biodiversity conservation. *Governance of Marine Fisheries and Biodiversity Conservation: Interaction and Coevolution*, 413–428.

Chatterton, P., Featherstone, D. and Routledge, P. (2013). Articulating climate justice in Copenhagen: Antagonism, the commons, and solidarity. *Antipode*, 45(3), 602–620.

Chuenpagdee, R., Degnbol, P., Bavinck, M., et al. (2005). Challenges and concerns in capture fisheries and aquaculture. *Fish for life: Interactive Governance for Fisheries*. Amsterdam, The Netherlands: Amsterdam University Press, 25–40.

Claeys, P., and Delgado Pugley, D. (2017). Peasant and indigenous transnational social movements engaging with climate justice. *Canadian Journal of Development Studies/Revue Canadienne d'études du développement*, 38(3), 325–340.

Claeys, P., and Duncan, J. (2019). Food sovereignty and convergence spaces. *Political Geography*, 75, 102045.

Claeys, P., and Edelman, M. (2020). The United Nations Declaration on the rights of peasants and other people working in rural areas. *The Journal of Peasant Studies*, 47(1), 1–68.

Clapp, J. (2014). Financialization, distance and global food politics. *The Journal of Peasant Studies*, 41(5), 797–814.

Clapp, J., and Moseley, W.G. (2020). This food crisis is different: COVID-19 and the fragility of the neoliberal food security order. *The Journal of Peasant Studies*, 47(7), 1393–1417.

Clapp, J., Newell, P., and Brent, Z.W. (2018). The global political economy of climate change, agriculture and food systems. *The Journal of Peasant Studies*, 45(1), 1–9.

Clark, B., and Clausen, R. (2008). The oceanic crisis: Capitalism and the degradation of marine ecosystems. *Monthly Review*, 60(3), 91–111.

Cooperation of People in Asia, Latin America and Africa. (1984). *International Conference of Fishworkers and their Supporters, Rome July 4–8 1984*. Report.

Costello, C., and Ovando, D. (2019). Status, institutions, and prospects for global capture fisheries. *Annual Review of Environment and Resources*, 44, 177–200.

CSM (Civil Society and Indigenous Peoples' Mechanism). (2021). What is the CSM? <https://www.csm4cfs.org/what-is-the-csm/>.

____. (2020). *CSM Annual Report 2019*. <https://www.csm4cfs.org/wp-content/uploads/2020/06/EN-CSM-AR-2020.pdf>.

Damanik, R. (2015). Fisherfolks are pushing the solution, not the illusion of blue carbon. Transnational Institute. <https://www.tni.org/en/article/fisherfolks-are-pushing-the-solution-not-the-illusion-of-blue-carbon>.

Das, L.K. (2018). Social movements–judicial activism Nexus and neoliberal transformation in India: Revisiting save Chilika movement. *Sociological Bulletin*, 67(1), 84–102.

De Schutter, O. (2012). *Interim Report of the Special Rapporteur on the Right to Food.* United Nations General Assembly.

De Silva, D.A.M., and Yamao, M. (2007). Effects of the tsunami on fisheries and coastal livelihood: A case study of tsunami-ravaged southern Sri Lanka. *Disasters*, 31(4), 386–404.

Diani, M. (2015). Social Movements, Networks and. *The Blackwell Encyclopedia of Sociology*. Wiley-Blackwell.

Dietz, T., Ostrom, E., and Stern, P.C. (2003). The struggle to govern the commons. *Science*, 302(5652), 1907–1912.

Dressler, W., Büscher, B., and Fletcher, R. (2014). The limits of Nature™ Inc. and the search for vital alternatives. In Büscher, B., Dressler, W., and Fletcher, R. (eds.), *Nature Inc.: Environmental Conservation in the Neoliberal Age*. Tucson: University of Arizona Press.

EC (European Commission). (2022). Sustainable fisheries partnership agreements (SFPAS). <https://oceans-and-fisheries.ec.europa.eu/fisheries/international-agreements/sustainable-fisheries-partnership-agreements-sfpas_en>.

European Parliament. (2020). The blue economy: Overview of the EU policy framework. <https://www.europarl.europa.eu/thinktank/en/document.html?reference=EPRS _IDA(2 020)646152>.

Edelman, M. (2009). Synergies and tensions between rural social movements and professional researchers. *The Journal of Peasant Studies*, 36(1), 245–265.

____. (2001). Social movements: Changing paradigms and forms of politics. *Annual Review of Anthropology*, 30(1), 285–317.

____. (1999). *Peasants against Globalization: Rural Social Movements in Costa Rica.* Redwood City: Stanford University Press.

Edelman, M., and Borras, S. (2016). *Political Dynamics of Transnational Agrarian Movement*. Agrarian Change and Peasant Studies series. Halifax: Fernwood Publishing.

Edelman, M., and James, C. (2011). Peasants' rights and the UN system: Quixotic struggle? Or emancipatory idea whose time has come? *The Journal of Peasant*

Studies, 38(1), 81–108.

Eikeset, A.M., Mazzarella, A.B., Davíðsdóttir, B., et al. (2018). What is blue growth? The semantics of "Sustainable Development" of marine environments. *Marine Policy*, 87, 177–179.

Ertör, I., and Ortega-Cerdà, M. (2018). The expansion of intensive marine aquaculture in Turkey: The next-to-last commodity frontier? *Journal of Agrarian Change*, 19(2), 1–24.

FAO (Food and Agriculture Organization of the United Nations). (2021a). The FAO SSF Umbrella Programme. <http://www.fao.org/voluntary-guidelines-small-scale-fisheries/implementation/umbrella-programme/en/>.

____. (2021b). Committee on Fisheries (COFI). <http://www.fao.org/about/meetings/cofi/en/>.

____. (2021c). Committee on Fisheries Thirty-fourth Session, Provisional Agenda. <http://www.fao.org/3/nc865en/nc865en.pdf>.

____. (2021d). Committee on World Food Security: CFS structure. <http://www.fao.org/cfs/about-cfs/cfs-structure/en/>.

____. (2021e). Climate-smart agriculture. <http://www.fao.org/climate-smart-agriculture/en/>.

____. (2020a). *Coastal Fisheries Initiative: Promoting Sustainable Fisheries in Coastal Areas*. Rome: FAO. <http://www.fao.org/fileadmin/user_upload/ common_oceans/CFI/docs/CFI_factsheet_2019.pdf>.

____. (2020b). About Us – Fisheries Division (NFI). <https://www.fao.org/fishery-aquaculture/en>.

____. (2020c). *The State of World Fisheries and Aquaculture: Sustainability in Action*. Rome: FAO.

____. (2020d). *The Impact of COVID-19 on Fisheries and Aquaculture Food Systems: Possibele Responses*. Information paper, November. Rome: FAO. <https://www.fao.org/documents/card/en/c/cb2537en/>.

____. (2019a). *The State of the World's Aquatic Genetic Resources for Food and Agriculture*. Rome: FAO.

____. (2019b). Committee on World Food Security (CFS) Forty-sixth Session: *Making a Difference in Food Security and Nutrition*. Report. Rome, 14–18 October. <https://www.fao.org/fileadmin/templates/cfs/Docs1819/cfs46/FinalReport/CFS46_Final_Report_EN.pdf>.

____. (2018a). FAO hails landmark UN resolution that enshrines rights of peasants and rural workers, 18 December. <http://www.fao.org/news/story/en/item/1175208/icode/>.

____. (2018b). *The State of World Fisheries and Aquaculture 2018: Meeting the Sustainable Development Goals*. Rome: FAO.

____. (2018c). Update on progress to develop the Global Strategic Framework (SSF-GSF) in Support of the Implementation of the SSF Guidelines. <https://www.fao.org/3/ca7737en/CA7737EN.pdf>.

____. (2018d). *Report of the Thirty-third Session of the Committee on Fisheries*. <https://www.fao.org/documents/card/en/c/ca5184en/>.

____. (2016). *The State of World Fisheries and Aquaculture 2016: Meeting the Sustainable Development Goals*. Rome: FAO.

____. (2015). *Voluntary Guidelines for Securing Sustainable Small-Scale Fisheries in the Context of Food Security and Poverty Eradication*. Rome: FAO. <https://www.fao.org/voluntary-guidelines-small-scale-fisheries/en/>.

____. (2014a). *Report of the Thirty-First Session on the Committee on Fisheries*. Rome, 9–13 June. Rome: FAO. <http://www.fao.org/3/i4634e/i4634e.pdf>.

____. (2014b). Nicole Franz – FAO Fisheries and Aquaculture Department. <http://www.fao.org/voluntary-guidelines-small-scale-fisheries/resources/detail/en/c/1196174/>.

____. (2013). In pursuit of securing the rights of fishing communities. (Interview with Rolf Willmann.) <http://www.fao.org/news/audio-video/detail-audio/en/?no_cache=1&uid=10135>.

____. (2012). *The State of World Fisheries and Aquaculture 2012: Meeting the Sustainable Development Goals*. Rome: FAO.

____. (2009). *Reform of the Committee on World Food Security: Final Version*. <http://www.fao.org/3/k7197e/k7197e.pdf>.

____. (2008). *Report of the Global Conference on Small-Scale Fisheries – Securing Sustainable Small-Scale Fisheries: Bringing Together Responsible Fisheries and Social Development*. Rome: FAO.

____. (1984). *Report of the FAO World Conference on Fisheries Management and Development*, Rome, 27 June to 6 July, 1984. Rome: FAO. <http://www.fao.org/publications/card/en/c/ 64859a7d-8c70-5e56-a042-b52f6bea7ea6/>.

Featherstone, D. (2013). The contested politics of climate change and the crisis of neo-liberalism. *ACME: An International Journal for Critical Geographies*, 12(1), 44–64.

Finley, C. (2016). The industrialization of commercial fishing, 1930–2016. In *Oxford Research Encyclopedia of Environmental Science*.

Fish Site. (2011). Fishermen's leaders speak out against aquaculture. <https://thefishsite.com/articles/fishermens-leaders-speak-out-against-aquaculture>.

Foley, P., and Mather, C. (2019). Ocean grabbing, terraqueous territoriality and social development. *Territory, Politics, Governance*, 7(3), 297–315.

Fox J. (2010). Coalitions and networks. In H.K. Anheier and S. Toepler (eds.), *International Encyclopedia of Civil Society*, 486–492. New York: Springer.

____. (2005). Unpacking "transnational citizenship." *Annual Review of Political Science*, 8, 171–201.

Fraser, N. (2021). Climates of capital for a trans-environmental eco-socialism. *New Left Review*, (127), 94–127.

Funge-Smith, S., and Bennett, A. (2019). A fresh look at inland fisheries and their role in food security and livelihoods. *Fish and Fisheries*, 20(6), 1176–1195.

Gasper, D. (2019). The road to the sustainable development goals: Building global alliances and norms. *Journal of Global Ethics*, 15(2), 118–137.

____. (2007). Human rights, human needs, human development, human security: Relationships between four international "human" discourses. *Forum for Development Studies*, 34(1), 9–43.

Gasper, D., Shah, A., and Tankha, S. (2019). The framing of sustainable consumption and production in SDG 12. *Global Policy*, 10, 83–95.

Gaventa, J. (2006). Finding the spaces for change: a power analysis. *IDS Bulletin*,

37(6), 23–33.

Gaventa, J., and Tandon, R. (2010) Citizen engagements in a globalizing world. In Gaventa, J. and Tandon, R. (eds.), *Globalizing Citizens: New Dynamics of Inclusion and Exclusion*. London: Zed Books, 3–30.

Greer, D., and Harvey, B. (2013). *Blue Genes: Sharing and Conserving the World's Aquatic Biodiversity*. Ottawa: International Development Research Centre.

GRtFN (Global Right to Food and Nutrition Network). (2015). The global convergence of land and water struggles. <https://www.righttofoodandnutrition.org/files/The%20Global%20Convergence%20of%20Land%20and%20Water%20Struggles.pdf>.

Gui, J.F., Tang, Q., Li, Z., et al. (eds.). (2018). *Aquaculture in China: Success Stories and Modern Trends*. Hoboken: John Wiley & Sons.

Guttal, S. (2020). Impacts of COVID-19 on small-scale and traditional fishers and fishworkers in India. *Focus on the Global South*, October 8. <https://focusweb.org/impacts-of-covid-19-on-small-scale-and-traditional-fishers-and-fishworkers-in-india/>.

Hardin, G. (1968). The tragedy of the commons. *Science*, 162(3859), 1243–1248.

Havice, E., Marschke, M., and Vandergeest, P. (2020). Industrial seafood systems in the immobilizing COVID-19 moment. *Agriculture and Human Values*, 37, 655–656.

HLPE (High Level Panel of Experts). (2020). *Impacts of COVID-19 on Food Security and Nutrition: Developing Effective Policy Responses to Address the Hunger and Malnutrition Pandemic*. Rome: FAO.<https://www.fao.org/3/cb1000en/cb1000en.pdf>.

Høst, J., (2015). *Market-Based Fisheries Management: Private Fish and Captains of Finance* (Vol. 16). New York: Springer.

Hunsberger, C., Corbera, E., Borras Jr, S.M., et al. (2017). Climate change mitigation, land grabbing and conflict: Towards a landscape-based and collaborative action research agenda. *Canadian Journal of Development Studies/Revue canadienne d'études du développement*, 38(3), 305–324.

Ibarra, A.A., Reid, C., and Thorpe, A. (2000). Neo-liberalism and its impact on overfishing and overcapitalisation in the marine fisheries of Chile, Mexico and Peru. *Food Policy*, 25(5), 599–622.

ICSF (International Collective in Support of Fishworkers). (1984–2021). ICSF Archives. <http://icsfarchives.net/>.

___. (2021). About ICSF. <https://www.icsf.net/about-icsf/>.

___. (2020). *Samudra Report, September 2020*. <https://www.icsf.net/samudra-articles.php?id=5364>.

ILO (International Labour Organization). (2021). International labour standards on fishers. <https://www.ilo.org/global/standards/subjects-covered-by-international-labour-standards/fishers/lang--en/index.htm>.

IPC (International Planning Committee for Food Sovereignty). (2021a). Working Group on Fisheries Statement on COVID-19. <https://www.foodsovereignty.org/ipc-working-group-on-fisheries-statement-on-covid-19/>.

___. (2021b). IPC statements to COFI34. <https://www.foodsovereignty.org/ipc-statements-to-cofi34/>.

____. (2019a). Fisheries working group. <https://www.foodsovereignty.org/working_groups/fisheries/>.

____. (2019b). Global Strategic Framework in support of the implementation of the SSF Guidelines. <https://www.foodsovereignty.org/ssf-gsf/>.

____. (2018). IPC Intervention on COFI Agenda Item 8.2: Small-Scale and Artisanal Fisheries Governance.

____. (2017). *IPC Handbook*. <https://www.foodsovereignty.org/ipc-handbook/>.

IPCC (Intergovernmental Panel on Climate Change). (2018). *Global Warming of 1.5°C*, Special Report. <https://www.ipcc.ch/site/assets/uploads/sites/2/2019/06/SR15_Full_Report_High_Res.pdf>.

Isaacs, M. (2019). Blue Justice for Small-Scale Fisheries. <https://www.plaas.org.za/blue-justice-for-small-scale-fisheries/>.

____. (2011). Individual transferable quotas, poverty alleviation and challenges for small country fisheries policy in South Africa. *MAST*, 10(2), 63–84.

Isaacs, M., and Hara, M. (2015). *Backing Small-Scale Fishers: Opportunities and Challenges in Transforming the Fish Sector*. Cape Town: PLAAS. <https://www.researchgate.net/publication/282655827_Backing_Small-Scale_Fisheries_Opportunities_and_Challenges_in_Transforming_the_Fish_Sector>.

Isaacs, M., and Witbooi, E. (2019). Fisheries crime, human rights and small-scale fisheries in South Africa: A case of bigger fish to fry. *Marine Policy*, 105, 158–168.

Jamwal, N. (2020). Lockdown enforced when they were at sea – so more than a lakh of fishers now wait in deep waters. *Goan Connection*, April 2. <https://en.gaonconnection.com/lockdown-enforced-when-they-were-at-sea-so-lakhs-of-fishers-now-wait-in-deep-waters/>.

Jentoft, S. (2019). *Life above Water: Essays on Human Experiences of Small-Scale Fisheries*. St. John's: TBTI Global.

Johnston, A. (1995–2012). Personal WFF and WFFP photo archive. First accessed in December 2019.

____. (1997). The Third World demands access. *South African Commerical Marine Magazine*, 6(4), December 1997 – February 1998.

Jones, R., Rigg, C., and Pinkerton, E. (2017). Strategies for assertion of conservation and local management rights: A Haida Gwaii herring story. *Marine Policy*, 80, 154–167.

Jordan, B. (2020). COVID-19: Inland fisheries plead with minister for "essential" status. *Times LIVE*, 28 March. <https://www.timeslive.co.za/news/south-africa/2020-03-28-covid-19-inland-fisheries-plead-with-minister-for-essential-status/>.

Kelleher, G., Bleakley, C. and Wells, S. (eds.). (1995). *A Global Representative System of Marine Protected Areas Vol. 3: Central Indian Ocean, Arabian Seas, East Africa and East Asian Seas*. Washington, DC: World Bank. <https://www.iucn.org/content/a-global-representative-system-marine-protected-areas-vol3>.

KNTI and WFFP (World Forum of Fisher Peoples). (2017). *Agroecology and Food Sovereignty in Small-Scale Fisheries*. Report. <https://www.tni.org/en/publication/agroecology-and-food-sovereignty-in-small-scale-fisheries>.

Krøvel, A.V., Gjerstad, B., Skoland, K., et al. (2019). Exploring attitudes toward aquaculture in Norway – Is there a difference between the Norwegian general public and local communities where the industry is established? *Marine Policy*, 108.

Kurien, J. (2007). The blessing of the commons: Small-scale fisheries, community property rights, and coastal natural assets. In Boyce, J.K., Narain, S., & Stanton, E.A. (eds.), *Reclaiming Nature: Environmental Justice and Ecological Restoration*. London: Anthem Press.

___. (2006). *Untangling Subsidies, Supporting Fisheries: The WTO Fisheries Subsidies Debate and Developing Country Priorities.* International Collective in Support of Fishworkers.

___. (1996). *Towards a new agenda for sustainable small-scale fisheries development.* Trivandrum: South Indian Federation of Fishermen Societies (SIFFS).

___. (1978). Entry of big business into fishing: its impact on fish economy. *Economic and Political Weekly*, 1557–1565.

Levkoe, C.Z. (2014) The food movement in Canada: A social movement network perspective. *The Journal of Peasant Studies*, 41(3), 385–403.

Levkoe, C.Z., Lowitt, K., and Nelson, C. (2017). "Fish as food": Exploring a food sovereignty approach to small-scale fisheries. *Marine Policy*, 85, 65–70.

Longo, S.B., Clausen, R., and Clark, B. (2015). *The Tragedy of the Commodity: Oceans, Fisheries, and Aquaculture.* New Brunswick: Rutgers University Press.

LVC (La Vía Campesina). (2021). The international peasants' voice. <https://viacampesina.org/en/international-peasants-voice/>.

___. (2017). *La Vía Campesina Annual Report 2017.* <https://viacampesina.org/en/la-via-campesina-2017-annual-report-is-out/>.

___. (2015a). Declaration of the global convergence of land and water struggles. April. <https://viacampesina.org/en/declaration-of-the-global-convergence-of-land-and-water-struggles/>.

___. (2015b). COP21: La Vía Campesina brings peasant voices to People's Climate Summit. <https://viacampesina.org/en/cop21-la-via-campesina-brings-peasant-voices-to-people-s-climate-summit/>.

___. (2007). Exposing false solutions, building real answers, climate justice for all. <https://focusweb.org/exposing-false-solutions-building-real-answersclimate-justice-for-all/>.

MacGinty, R. (2012). Between resistance and compliance: Nonparticipation and the Liberal peace. *Journal of Intervention and Statebuilding*, 6(2), 167–187.

Mallin, F., and Barbesgaard, M. (2020). Awash with contradiction: Capital, ocean space and the logics of the Blue Economy Paradigm. *Geoforum*, 113, 121–132.

Mallin, M.A.F., Stolz, D.C., Thompson, B.S. and Barbesgaard, M. (2019). In oceans we trust: Conservation, philanthropy, and the political economy of the Phoenix Islands Protected Area. *Marine Policy*, 107, 103421.

Mansfield, B. (2011). "Modern" industrial fisheries and the crisis of overfishing. In R. Peet, P. Robbins and M. Watts (eds.), *Global Political Ecology*, 84–99. London: Routledge.

Marchetti, R. (2017). International policy partnerships with civil society: Risks and opportunities. In *Partnerships in International Policy-Making*, 3–30. London: Palgrave Macmillan.

Marschke, M., Vandergeest, P., Havice, E., et al. (2021). COVID-19, instability and migrant fish workers in Asia. *Maritime Studies*, 20(1), 87–99.

Martinez-Alier, J., L. Temper, L. Del Bene, D., and Scheidel, A. (2016). Is there a global environmental justice movement? *The Journal of Peasant Studies*, 43(3), 731–755.

McAdam, D. (1995). "Initiator" and "spin-off" movements: Diffusion processes in protest cycles. In M. Traugott (ed.), *Repertoires and Cycles of Collective Action*, 217–239. Duke University Press.

MCI (Marine Conservation Institute). (2022). 30x30: Protecting at least 30% of the ocean by 2030. <https://marine-conservation.org/30x30/>.

McKeon, N. (2017a). Civil society-public institution relations in global food policy: The case of FAO and the CFS. In R. Marchetti (ed.), *Partnerships in International Policy-Making*, 71–88. London: Palgrave Macmillan.

____. (2017b). Are equity and sustainability a likely outcome when foxes and chickens share the same coop? Critiquing the concept of multistakeholder governance of food security. *Globalizations*, 14(3), 379–398.

____. (2013). "One does not sell the land upon which the people walk": Land grabbing, transnational rural social movements, and global governance. *Globalizations*, 10(1), 105–122.

Mendez, J. B. (2008). Globalizing scholar activism: Opportunities and dilemmas through a feminist lens. In C. Hale (ed.), *Engaging Contradictions: Theory, Politics, and Methods of Activist Scholarship*, 136–163. Oakland: University of California Press.

Menon, A., Sowman, M., and Bavinck, M. (2018). Rethinking capitalist transformation of fisheries in South Africa and India. *Ecology and Society*, 23(4).

Mills, E.N. (2022). Transnational fishers' movements: emergence, evolution, and contestation. *Maritime Studies*, 1–18.

____. (2021). The politics of transnational fishers' movements. *The Journal of Peasant Studies*, 1–26.

____. (2018). Implicating "fisheries justice" movements in food and climate politics. *Third World Quarterly*, 39(7), 1–20.

Mills, E., Rinder Alexandersen, A., Barbesgaard, M., et al. (2017). *EU Fisheries Agreements: Cheap Fish for a High Price*. Report published by the Transnational Institute (TNI). <https://www.tni.org/files/publication-downloads/tni_eu_fisheries_agreements_en.pdf>.

Nakamura, J., Chuenpagdee, R., and El Halimi, M. (2021). Unpacking legal and policy frameworks: A step ahead for implementing the Small-Scale Fisheries Guidelines. *Marine Policy*, 129, 104568.

Nayak, P. K., and Berkes, F. (2010). Whose marginalisation? Politics around environmental injustices in India's Chilika lagoon. *Local Environment*, 15(6), 553–567.

Nellemann, C., Corcoran, E., Duarte, C.M., et al. (eds.). (2009). *Blue Carbon: The Role of Healthy Oceans in Binding Carbon. A Rapid Response Assessment*. United Nations Environment Programme. <https://ccom.unh.edu/sites/default/files/publications/Nellemann_2010_BlueCarbon_book.pdf>.

Newell, P. (2011). Civil society and accountability in the global governance of climate change. In Scholte (ed.), *Building Global Democracy: Civil Society and*

Accountable Global Governance, (225–244).

Nyéléni (2007). *Declaration of Nyéléni.* <https://nyeleni.org/IMG/pdf/DeclNyeleni-en.pdf>.

O'Connor, J. (1998). *Natural Causes: Essays in Ecological Marxism.* New York: Guilford Press.

O'Riordan, B. (2000). Troubled seas in Loctudy. *Samudra*, 27. Chennai: ICSF.

OceanCare. (2020). Informing global policies to reduce ocean noise for the benefit of marine life protection and the sustainability of global fisheries. <https://sdgs.un.org/partnerships/informing-global-policies-reduce-ocean-noise-benefit-marine-life-protection-and>.

Ocean Foundation. (2021). Sustainable aquaculture project. <https://oceanfdn.org/projects/sustainable-aquaculture/>.

OECD (Organisation for Economic Co-operation and Development). (2010). *Globalisation in Fisheries and Aquaculture: Opportunities and Challenges.* Paris: OECD.

Olin Wright, E. (2019). *How to Be an Anticapitalist in the Twenty-First Century.* London: Verso Books.

Orr, S.K. (2016). Institutional control and climate change activism at COP 21 in Paris. *Global Environmental Politics*, 16(3), 23–30.

Ostrom, E. (1990). *Governing the commons: The evolution of institutions for collective action.* Cambridge: Cambridge University Press.

Pictou, S. (2017). The origins and politics, campaigns and demands by the international fisher peoples' movement: An Indigenous perspective. *Third World Quarterly*, 39(7), 1–10.

____. (2015). Small 't' treaty relationships without borders: Bear River First Nation, clam harvesters, the Bay of Fundy Marine Resources Centre and the World Forum of Fisher Peoples. *Anthropologica*, 57(2), 457–467. <https://www.jstor.org/stable/26350454>.

Pinkerton, E. (2017). Hegemony and resistance: Disturbing patterns and hopeful signs in the impact of neoliberal policies on small-scale fisheries around the world. *Marine Policy*, 80, 1–9.

Prasertcharoensuk, R., and Shott, J. (2010). *Time for a Sea Change: A Study of the Effectiveness of Biodiversity Conservation Measures and Marine Protected Areas Along Southern Thailand's Andaman Sea Coastline.* Chennai: ICSF. <https://aquadocs.org/bitstream/handle/1834/21840/mpa_thailand.pdf?sequence=1>.

Prendergast, J. (2020). Coronavirus likely to wipe $389 million off Australian seafood industry's bottom line. ABC News, 4 March. <https://www.abc.net.au/news/2020-03-05/australian-seafood-takes-massive-hit-as-coronavirus-spreads/12022136>.

Protected Planet. (2020). Explore the world's marine protected areas. <https://www.protectedplanet.net/en/thematic-areas/marine-protected-areas>.

Pullin, R.S. (2008). Management of aquatic biodiversity and genetic resources. *Reviews in Fisheries Science*, 8(4), 379–393.

Ratner, B.D., Åsgård, B., and Allison, E.H. (2014). Fishing for justice: Human rights, development, and fisheries sector reform. *Global Environmental Change*, 27, 120–130.

Rigby, B., Davis, R., Bavington, D., and Baird, C. (2017). Industrial aquaculture and the politics of resignation. *Marine Policy*, 80, 19–27.
Rivera-Ferre, M.G., Constance, D.H., and Renard, M.C. (2014). Convergence and divergence in alternative agrifood movements. In D.H. Constance, M.C. Renard and M.G. Rivera-Ferre (eds.), *Alternative Agrifood Movements: Patterns of Convergence and Divergence*. Emerald Group Publishing Limited.
Robbins, M.J. (2015). Exploring the 'localisation' dimension of food sovereignty. *Third World Quarterly*, 36(3), 449–468.
Ronquest-Ross, L.C., Vink, N. and Sigge, G.O. (2015). Food consumption changes in South Africa since 1994. *South African Journal of Science*, 111(9–10), 1–12.
Rosset, P. (2013). Re-thinking agrarian reform, land and territory in La Vía Campesina. *The Journal of Peasant Studies*, 40(4), 721–775.
Rosset, P., and Martinez-Torres, M.E. (2014). Food sovereignty and agroecology in the convergence of rural social movements.' In D.H. Constance, M.C. Renard and M.G. Rivera-Ferre (eds.), *Alternative Agrifood Movements: Patterns of Convergence and Divergence*. Emerald Group Publishing Ltd.
Saguin, K. (2016). Blue revolution in a commodity frontier: Ecologies of aquaculture and agrarian change in Laguna Lake, Philippines. *Journal of Agrarian Change*, 16(4), 571–593.
Sall, A., Belliveau, M., and Nayak, N. (2002). *Conversations: A Trialogue on Organization, Power and Intervention in Fisheries*. Chennai: ICSF.
Santiago, S. (2001). Wag the dog… A response to Mr. Brian O'Riordan's article entitled "Troubled seas in Loctudy." *Samudra*, 28. Chennai: ICSF.
Scheidel, A. (2019). Carbon stock indicators: reductionist assessments and contentious policies on land use. *The Journal of Peasant Studies*, 46(5), 913–934.
Scholte, J.A. (ed.). (2011). *Building Global Democracy? Civil Society and Accountable Global Governance*. Cambridge University Press.
Scott, J.C. (2008). *Weapons of the Weak*. New Haven: Yale University Press.
Segi, S. (2014). Protecting or pilfering? Neoliberal conservationist marine protected areas in the experience of coastal Granada, the Philippines. *Human Ecology*, 42(4), 565–575.
Silver, J.J., Gray, N.J., Campbell, L.M., et al. (2015). Blue economy and competing discourses in international oceans governance. *The Journal of Environment & Development*, 24(2), 135–160.
Singleton, R.L., Allison, E.H., Le Billon, P., and Sumaila, U.R. (2017). Conservation and the right to fish: International conservation NGOs and the implementation of the voluntary guidelines for securing sustainable small-scale fisheries. *Marine Policy*, 84, 22–32.
Sinha, S. (2012). Transnationality and the Indian Fishworkers' Movement, 1960s–2000. *Journal of Agrarian Change*, 12(2–3), 364–389.
Smith, J. (2013). Transnational social movements. *The Wiley-Blackwell Encyclopedia of Social and Political Movements*. Hoboken: Blackwell Publishing Ltd.
____. (1998). Characteristics of the modern transnational social movement sector. In J. Smith, C. Chatfield, and R. Pagnucco (eds.), *Transnational Social Movements and Global Politics: Solidarity Beyond the State*, 42–58.
Smith, M.P., and Guarnizo, L.E. (eds.). (2006). *Transnationalism from Below:*

Comparative Urban and Community Research, Volume 6. London: Transaction Publishers.

Song, A.M., and Soliman, A. (2019). Situating human rights in the context of fishing rights – contributions and contradictions. *Marine Policy,* 103, 19–26.

Steinberg, P.E. (1999). The maritime mystique: Sustainable development, capital mobility, and nostalgia in the world ocean. *Environment and Planning D: Society and Space,* 17(4), 403–426.

Sundar, A. (2012). Alternatives to crisis: Social movements in global fisheries governance. *Human Geography,* 5(2), 55–71.

Tarrow, S. (2011). *Power in Movement: Social Movements and Contentious Politics.* Updated and revised 3rd edition. Cambridge University Press.

____. (2005). *The New Transnational Activism.* Cambridge: Cambridge University Press.

TBTI (Too Big to Ignore). (2019). *Blue Justice for Small-Scale Fisheries.* <http://toobigtoignore.net/blue-justice-for-ssf/>.

____. (2015). Nicole Franz. Member profile and interview. <http://toobigtoignore.net/members/nicole-franz/>.

Thomas, S. (2014). Blue carbon: Knowledge gaps, critical issues, and novel approaches. *Ecological Economics,* 107, 22–38.

Tilly, C. (2004). *Social Movements, 1768–2004.* London: Paradigm Publishers.

TNI (Transnational Institute). (2014). *The Global Ocean Grab: A Primer.* <https://www.tni.org/en/publication/the-global-ocean-grab-a-primer>.

Tramel, S. (2018). Convergence as political strategy: social justice movements, natural resources and climate change. *Third World Quarterly,* 39(7), 1290–1307.

____. (2016). The road through Paris: Climate change, carbon, and the political dynamics of convergence. *Globalizations,* 13(6), 960–969.

____. (2015a). Sustainable development goals. <https://sdgs.un.org/goals>.

____. (2015b). *Paris Agreement.* Paris: United Nations. <https://unfccc.int/sites/default/files/english_paris_agreement.pdf>.

____. (2000). Millennium development goals. <https://www.un.org/millenniumgoals/bkgd.shtml>.

UNCLOS (United Nations Convention on the Law of the Seas). (1982). <https://www.un.org/depts/los/convention_agreements/convention_overview_convention.htm>.

UNFCCC (United National Framework Convention on Climate Change). (2021a). Conference of the Parties (COP). <https://unfccc.int/process/bodies/supreme-bodies/conference-of-the-parties-cop>.

____. (2021b). Interim nationally determined contributions (NDC) registry. <https://www4.unfccc.int/sites/NDCStaging/Pages/All.aspx>.

____. (2021c). Processes and meetings: Non-party stakeholders. <https://unfccc.int/process-and-meetings/what-are-parties-non-party-stakeholders>.

____. (2021d). Warsaw framework for REDD+. <https://unfccc.int/topics/land-use/resources/warsaw-framework-for-redd-plus>.

Uson, M.A.M. (2017). Natural disasters and land grabs: The politics of their intersection in the Philippines following super typhoon Haiyan. *Canadian Journal of Development Studies/Revue canadienne d'études du développement,* 38(3),

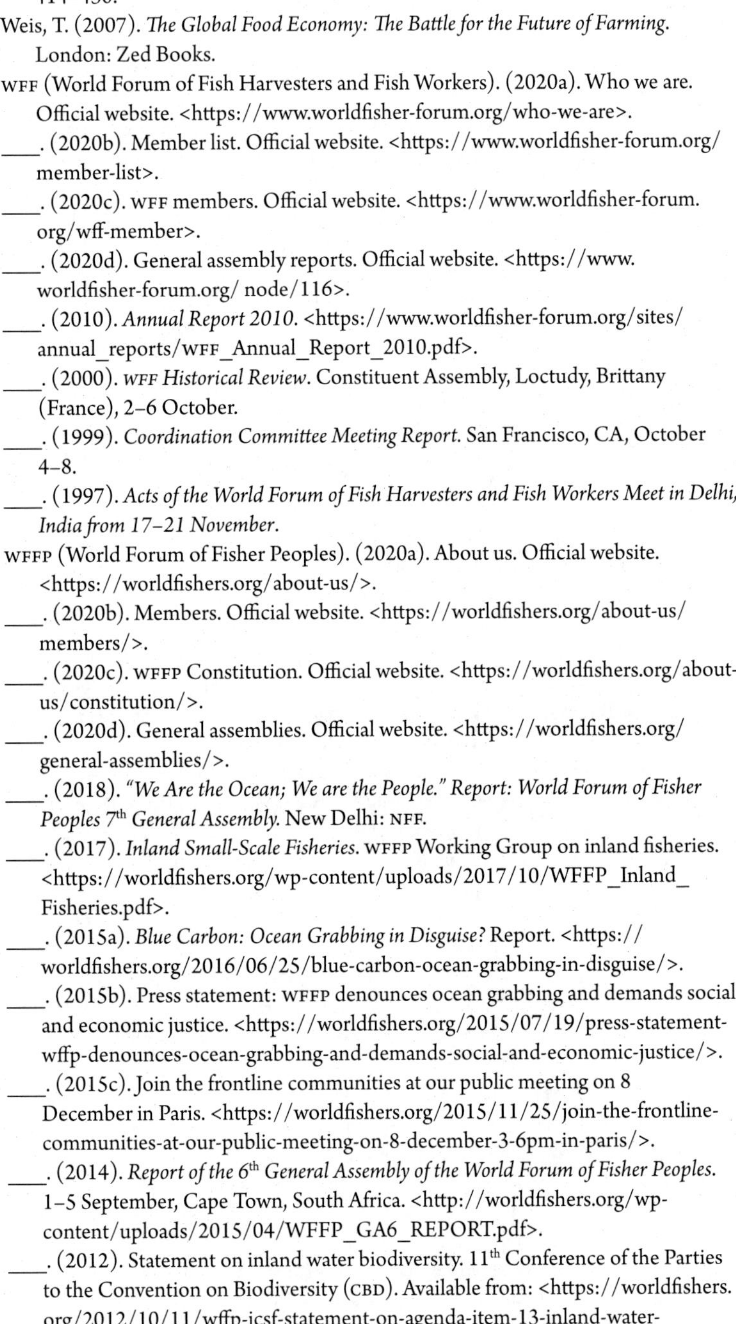

414–430.

Weis, T. (2007). *The Global Food Economy: The Battle for the Future of Farming.* London: Zed Books.

WFF (World Forum of Fish Harvesters and Fish Workers). (2020a). Who we are. Official website. <https://www.worldfisher-forum.org/who-we-are>.

____. (2020b). Member list. Official website. <https://www.worldfisher-forum.org/member-list>.

____. (2020c). WFF members. Official website. <https://www.worldfisher-forum.org/wff-member>.

____. (2020d). General assembly reports. Official website. <https://www.worldfisher-forum.org/ node/116>.

____. (2010). *Annual Report 2010.* <https://www.worldfisher-forum.org/sites/annual_reports/WFF_Annual_Report_2010.pdf>.

____. (2000). *WFF Historical Review.* Constituent Assembly, Loctudy, Brittany (France), 2–6 October.

____. (1999). *Coordination Committee Meeting Report.* San Francisco, CA, October 4–8.

____. (1997). *Acts of the World Forum of Fish Harvesters and Fish Workers Meet in Delhi, India from 17–21 November.*

WFFP (World Forum of Fisher Peoples). (2020a). About us. Official website. <https://worldfishers.org/about-us/>.

____. (2020b). Members. Official website. <https://worldfishers.org/about-us/members/>.

____. (2020c). WFFP Constitution. Official website. <https://worldfishers.org/about-us/constitution/>.

____. (2020d). General assemblies. Official website. <https://worldfishers.org/general-assemblies/>.

____. (2018). *"We Are the Ocean; We are the People." Report: World Forum of Fisher Peoples 7th General Assembly.* New Delhi: NFF.

____. (2017). *Inland Small-Scale Fisheries.* WFFP Working Group on inland fisheries. <https://worldfishers.org/wp-content/uploads/2017/10/WFFP_Inland_Fisheries.pdf>.

____. (2015a). *Blue Carbon: Ocean Grabbing in Disguise?* Report. <https://worldfishers.org/2016/06/25/blue-carbon-ocean-grabbing-in-disguise/>.

____. (2015b). Press statement: WFFP denounces ocean grabbing and demands social and economic justice. <https://worldfishers.org/2015/07/19/press-statement-wffp-denounces-ocean-grabbing-and-demands-social-and-economic-justice/>.

____. (2015c). Join the frontline communities at our public meeting on 8 December in Paris. <https://worldfishers.org/2015/11/25/join-the-frontline-communities-at-our-public-meeting-on-8-december-3-6pm-in-paris/>.

____. (2014). *Report of the 6th General Assembly of the World Forum of Fisher Peoples.* 1–5 September, Cape Town, South Africa. <http://worldfishers.org/wp-content/uploads/2015/04/WFFP_GA6_REPORT.pdf>.

____. (2012). Statement on inland water biodiversity. 11th Conference of the Parties to the Convention on Biodiversity (CBD). Available from: <https://worldfishers.org/2012/10/11/wffp-icsf-statement-on-agenda-item-13-inland-water-

biodiversity/>.

___. (2008). Bangkok civil society statement on small-scale fisheries. <https://worldfishers.org/2008/10/17/bangkok-civil-society-statement-small-scale-fisheries-2/>.

___. (2001). *General Secretary's Report to the World Forum of Fisher Peoples (WFFP) Coordination Committee, March 6–10 2001, Mumbai, India.*

WFFP (World Forum of Fisher Peoples), Afrika Kontakt and TNI (Transnational Institute). (2016). *Human Rights vs. Property Rights: Implementation and Interpretation of the SSF Guidelines.* <http://worldfishers.org/2016/12/19/human-rights-vs-property-rights-implementation-and-interpretation-of-the-ssf-guidelines/>.

WFFP (World Forum of Fisher Peoples) and WFF (World Forum of Fish Harvesters and Fish Workers). (2015a). No to blue carbon, yes to food sovereignty and climate justice! Statement issued in relation to the COP21 negotiations in Paris, 2015. <http://worldfishers.org/wp-content/uploads/2015/12/Blue_Carbon_Statement.pdf>

___. (2015b). Fisherfolks say no to the Coastal Fisheries Initiative. Joint press statement. <https://worldfishers.org/2015/11/09/fisherfolks-say-no-to-the-coastal-fisheries-initiative/>.

Wilhelm, T.A., Sheppard, C.R., Sheppard, A.L., et al. (2014). Large marine protected areas – advantages and challenges of going big. *Aquatic Conservation: Marine and Freshwater Ecosystems*, 24(S2), 24–30.

Wolff, M. (2015). From sea sharing to sea sparing – Is there a paradigm shift in ocean management? *Ocean & Coastal Management*, 116, 58–63.

World Bank. (2013). *Fish to 2030: Prospects for Fisheries and Aquaculture.* World Bank Report Number 83177. <https://documents.worldbank.org/en/publication/documents-reports/documentdetail/458631468152376668/fish-to-2030-prospects-for-fisheries-and-aquaculture>.

Index